College Match:
A Blueprint for Choosing the Best School for You!

Fourth Edition

by
Steven R. Antonoff, Ph.D.
Marie A. Friedemann, Ph.D.

Cover Design by Supon Design
Book Design by Edington-Rand

© 1995 by Steven R. Antonoff and Marie A. Friedemann
All Rights Reserved

Care and diligence have been taken in preparing the data contained herein, however, Octameron does not guarantee its accuracy.

Address correspondence to:
Octameron Associates
PO Box 2748
Alexandria, VA 22301
703/836-5480

Address bookstore inquiries regarding purchases and returns to:
Dearborn Trade
155 North Wacker Drive
Chicago, IL 60606-1719
312/836-4400
Outside Illinois, 800/245-BOOK

ISBN 1-57509-004-X
PRINTED IN THE UNITED STATES OF AMERICA

CONTENTS

Preface

College Match is intended for use as a workbook and guide in the process of choosing a college. As practicing professionals, we have used, tested and refined the information and materials in this workbook throughout the last fifteen years of our work with students. We wrote this book because we found no other guidebook or set of materials that systematically and comprehensively aided the process of choice. It does not pretend to have all the answers to the issues faced by prospective college students and their families. But it does, we believe, provide perspective and guidance and, further, gives college shoppers a framework upon which to base solid choices.

Four important perspectives are central to this book.

First, we believe all students, regardless of grades or test scores, have colleges from which to choose. Students merely need to seize the opportunity and realize that choices do exist. Through the use of this book, along with proper guidance and support, all students will find colleges where they will be successful. After all, the collegiate opportunities in the United States are tremendous.

Second, we believe the college choice process neither has to be, nor is inherently, stressful. While some students and their parents are anxious about selecting a college, we believe much of that stress comes from false assumptions about the nature of college admission. Once students and their families replace the quest for "the best college" with one focusing on "the best fit," the level of tension will be reduced significantly. While this book covers both "getting in" and "fitting in," it focuses on "fitting in" because we feel this is the primary emphasis throughout the college selection process.

Third, we believe there is a sequence of steps which, if followed, will lead to solid, suitable college choices. This book is organized around those steps. Systematically moving from one step to the next will lead to self and college awarenesses. These awarenesses are the "stuff" upon which college choices should be based.

Fourth, we believe that finding a college builds important, lifelong skills in initiative-taking, decision-making and responsibility. For many students, choosing a college is their first real test of using values, personal preferences and feelings to make a real-life choice. By making difficult decisions during the college choice process, and accepting the consequences of their decisions, students will also gain a great deal of self-understanding.

This fourth edition includes several features about which we are particularly proud. The book's interactive nature, particularly the inclusion of the worksheets, enables students to participate actively in choosing a college. Such involvement, we have found, leads to better, more satisfying decisions. The "Self-Survey for the College Bound," the central component of Chapter 2, is the first attempt, of which we are aware, to aid students in understanding qualities about themselves and then to link those qualities to college choices. The materials included in Chapter 3 allow students to appreciate the impact of such qualities as size and location on their adjustment and college success. Overall, we feel *College Match* offers students encouragement (laced with realism) throughout the entire college choice process. When students are empowered with the knowledge that they have real options from which to choose their futures, they will feel confident and positive.

This book was inspired by the hundreds of students with whom we have worked over the last fifteen years. They have helped us in the preparation of these pages. Every worksheet has benefitted from the critical eyes of our students. More importantly, each student has, in his or her own way, opened our eyes to another issue, another possibility, another frame of reference involved in college choice. We have learned from each of them and, if our perspective is on-target, it is the result of their contributions to our thinking. And because we are always learning ourselves, we want to know the extent to which this book works for our current readers.

This edition is dedicated to the memory of our friend and colleague Eleanor Turner who assisted us in typing, proofing and modifying. We miss her.

As you begin choosing colleges, we hope you do so with openness and with enthusiasm. Also, we hope you will know the power of choice, and with it, you will choose schools where the best in you will be revealed.

We are anxious for your feedback and encourage you to write us at 875 South Colorado Boulevard, Suite 707, Denver, Colorado 80222.

Steven R. Antonoff, Ph.D.
Marie A. Friedemann, Ph.D.
Denver, Colorado
September, 1995

To Parents:
How to Use this Book

This book is written for students because we believe students should assume responsibility for the college search. But we are sensitive to the depth of parental concern about the college selection process, and we have written the book so that parents can play an important role, too. The following tips will guide you through these pages.

Parents should read Chapters 1 and 8 first. These two chapters provide important perspectives about the college search.

You can assist your student by encouraging him or her to move, sequentially, through the chapters. The chapters are organized according to the way the process of college planning most logically unfolds. Students should read one chapter at a time, completing any worksheets in that chapter. Chapters 2, 3 and 4 present the most central material and, thus, more time should be spent on them. Of course, there may be reasons to alter the order. If, for example, you are planning to visit college campuses, you should read Chapter 5 immediately. If your student is worried about college essays, he or she will find help in Chapter 6.

College Match includes thirteen worksheets, each building on the preceding one. Parents can review the worksheets after each is complete, adding insights as necessary. Each has a specific purpose. For example, Worksheet 2 enables the student to better understand himself or herself as an upcoming college student. Worksheet 5 delineates the factors your student believes to be important in choosing a college. Worksheet 5 should be shared and discussed as a family, and parents should not hesitate to add factors you feel should be considered in the process of college selection. Some of the worksheets are personal and ask the student to probe his or her background and readiness for college. Such self-assessment can be difficult, and some students find sharing these kinds of personal insights with anyone, parents included, awkward. But a nonjudgmental attitude and trust will go a long way toward better communication.

The following general guidelines/suggestions may be useful:

1. Students should be encouraged to take the college planning process seriously. It is neither a game nor an exercise. It is a process of thinking, reflecting, researching and choosing. And it takes time. You can't expect to find a college in a day. It is often laborious, and patience is as necessary here as it was when your child learned to walk or ride a bicycle.

2. Students need to understand the ambiguity that is always present in making important decisions. In the case of finding a college, there are no absolutes, few "rights" or "wrongs," and lots of conflicting information. Parents can assist their student by stressing that a solid college choice will be made if he or she methodically moves from one phase of college identification to the next.

3. Parents, like their students, should seek the help of experienced counselors. A competent and sensitive counselor will bring clarity as well as knowledge to your college shopping—and may defuse many familial conflicts, as well. Most importantly, the counselor, using the results of the worksheets in this book, is vital in identifying appropriate colleges for consideration.

4. Students are encouraged throughout the book to seek the opinions and perspectives of their parents about different topics. But you may want to give your student a gentle nudge every now and then to share viewpoints and feelings. We hope the book opens lines of communication and gives both parents and students a useful base of knowledge. We advise you to set aside one hour per week to talk about college planning issues.

5. Throughout the process, attempt to support your son's or daughter's good research skills. Good research includes asking lots of questions, reading, examining oneself and separating college facts from college lore. Help your student use the resources outlined in Chapter 4.

6. Expect a lot from your student, but be mindful of the difficulty of the teenage years. Adolescence is a time of conflicting feelings and perspectives; simultaneously, teenagers are independent and dependent, mature and child-like, all-knowing and yet knowing nothing. At one minute, they are ready to leave for college and yet desirous of the security of home and family. Take time to discuss these issues and feelings as they arise.

You have in your hands a blueprint for finding a college. Armed with this information, you should feel empowered to guide your student competently through the process.

A Note to Counselors

Although this book is directed at students and parents, we have written as counselors ourselves, and we have written because we believe in your role in the college search. The voice of an experienced counselor makes our words come alive to the college-bound student. And you will note that we have often directed the student to seek your counsel.

Unlike the outlook presented in some of the books on the market, we contend that the college planning and admission processes are not characterized by easy answers, fool-proof formulae, or sure-fire strategies. This is not a book of suggestions for "packaging" an applicant whose only goal is to "get in" to a "name brand" college. Because it provides neither recipes nor guarantees, it is, we believe, more in keeping with the way the college admission process, indeed life itself, unfolds. And, hopefully, it is more in keeping with your own philosophy.

We do believe this book can be used in busy guidance offices. In fact, it could serve as a student text for a course in college planning or a series of workshops for juniors and seniors. Also, the material is equally suitable for one-on-one meetings.

While the topics proceed in sequence, the chapters need not necessarily be used in the order in which they are laid out here; indeed, each guidance office will determine the suitability of the chapters (and the worksheets) according to the needs and goals of its own counseling program and the specific population of students that it serves.

Perhaps most importantly, however, this book is designed to maximize your time. Students who use the worksheets and read the text will come to you having reflected on themselves as well as those factors or qualities important in their college choice. They will come to you having given thought to essays or visits or other matters. And, having used the worksheets with hundreds of our own students, we believe them to be "student friendly"—with questions, instructions and interpretations that are self-explanatory and even interesting. When students come to you with this preparation and content, your time with each student can be utilized meaningfully on the most salient college counseling issues.

We have learned much from the writings and the practices of the many public and private school counselors with whom we have worked. This book reflects those insights, but our desire to learn continues. We are anxious to hear your opinions on the issues raised in the book and on the ways in which those issues are developed. Our address is found in the Preface.

The world of higher education is a rich one indeed, and we (public or private school counselors and educational consultants alike) share in the mission of opening up each student's eyes to that world. We hope this book contributes to that mission.

Chapter 1

Your Power to Choose A College

This is a book about choice. Choice is not a simple word. Our lives are filled with an endless array of choices. We ask such questions as: What will I wear today? Should I strive for A's and B's or be comfortable with B's and C's? What will I have for lunch? What book will I read? What courses should I take in school during my senior year? How much commitment do I want to make to sports or to my school work? Will I be gruff or kind to my friends today? Some choices are relatively simple, others are quite complex. Some affect our lives in a major way, others have few consequences. We make hundreds of choices in the span of even a single day. And not making a choice is a choice as well! The consequences of our choices can be good or they can be bad. They can be positive or they can be negative.

Picking a college is an important choice—perhaps the most important choice you have ever made. Your choice of a college can either be good or bad, positive or negative, depending upon your willingness to devote yourself to the process. If you invest yourself in the search, you will find many schools from which to choose. If you are passive and wait for your counselor or your parents or your mailbox to bring word of "the perfect school," chances are you'll be sadly disappointed with your ultimate choice.

So much has been written about "getting in" to college that students often seem surprised when the word "choice" is associated with college planning. Today, almost every student, regardless of academic record or family resources, can experience the joy of choosing from a wide variety of schools. Perhaps the most difficult task is truly believing you have the power to do so. Are you ready to begin the exciting process of making college choices?

Students often feel their choice of colleges is extremely limited. If they have not received all A's, if their high school classes are not the most competitive offered, or if their scores on standardized tests are below average, they may feel they do not or will not have choices—or at least that they will not get into a "good" college. How wrong these students are. First, as you will see, the definition of a "good" college is terribly subjective and imprecise. It tends to mean colleges about which you or your family have heard. But of the 3,000 or so colleges in the United States, with how many is a typical family really familiar? Very few. Second, however you choose to define "good," hundreds of "good colleges" exist. So be free to explore. Open yourself up to discovery.

There is a reverse side to the phenomenon just described. Instead of feeling they have too few choices, some students feel they have too many.

Parents are often enthusiastic and thrilled by all these choices. A student, however, may be confused and even believe "it would be better if I didn't have a choice." The process can become frustrating, especially since as students, you may be just learning the skills and strategies necessary to make good decisions. Just remember, at the beginning of the college search, your task may seem overwhelming, but, with patience and perseverance, your early frustration will pass, and ultimately, result in better college choices.

Your first choice is whether you desire a college education. Some students simply assume they will go to college and do not go through the important process of contemplating their lives without a college education. Many business and corporate leaders, to take one segment of society, do not have college degrees. Yet, they are happy and often financially successful. Be assertive in making your decision to go to college. Articulate why you want to go. It's not enough to say, "I need a college degree to get ahead." Instead, you should have the desire to learn; there should be subjects about which you want to know more. Articulating the values of a college education will enable you to appreciate the benefits of your education. To aid your thinking, make a list of the outcomes you desire from a college education. Think about how you want to be different as a result of going to college.

Another choice involves deciding whether you want to be a student. Often, students claim they want to go to college, yet they don't show the requisite commitment to the academic side of college life. They may see college as four years of fun and games. While college is filled with a great many social opportunities, college attendance is primarily an academic decision. Are you ready to make a commitment to your studies? Do you have the persistence necessary to be a successful student? Firmly deciding to be a student is important as you contemplate college attendance.

Assuming you're committed to pursuing a college education and to being a student, your next choice is when you want that education to begin. Some students delay the start of their college experience for a year or more to be prepared fully—emotionally as well as intellectually—for the rigors of college education. Many students spend productive years traveling, working or even pursuing hobbies. And research shows that students who take a year or so between their high school experience and the start of their college career are better prepared to meet the challenges of their college years. Still other students make the choice to begin their education at a two-year college, developing basic skills and confidence, before entering a four-year college. And there are students for whom a trade, vocational or technical school fits their needs perfectly.

You may feel several emotions as you embark on the task of selecting a college. You may feel happy with your successes in high school and look forward to four wonderful years in college. You may feel regret or anger that you didn't earn higher grades in high school. You may feel terror or panic at the complexity of finding a college that meets your background and personality. You may feel overwhelmed because there are so many colleges from which to choose. Or, you may feel more than one of these sentiments. Finding a college should not and need not be traumatic or stressful. You can look at your college choices in a positive or in a negative way. Let's take an example. Suppose Lucy is told she can probably get accepted to 2,900 of the possible 3,000 colleges in the United States. If Lucy is prone to negativism, she would say, "Heck, I can't get into 100 colleges and I'm depressed and angry." Instead, she should look at this situation in the appropriate, positive way and say, "Wow, 2,900 colleges want me and I can be successful at all of them!" Optimism and perspective are important as you begin to look for a college. Remember, 90% of the colleges in the U.S. accept over 80% of those who apply.

The diversity and excellence of United States colleges are truly mind-boggling. In fact, our colleges are widely regarded as the best developed in the world. Your investment in the college selection process is the first way to demonstrate your commitment to your future success. It's a unique opportunity to affect your life in a positive way.

COLLEGE CHOICE AS A PROCESS

Picking a collegiate atmosphere in which to spend four years is best viewed as a process, a series of steps in which each builds on the previous one. It is necessary to take your time and carefully complete each step before moving on to the next. That is the way this book is designed. You start with an analysis of yourself as a potential college student. You then review the qualities that will make a college right for you. You next use all of the resources at your disposal to select the colleges to which you will apply. Finally, after hearing from your colleges, you move to the last step: picking your college.

The essential premise of this book is that by going through the steps as outlined, you will have excellent colleges from which to choose. But you need to be an active participant in the process. You need to take your selection of a college seriously. You have to be open to new information and put aside any stereotypes or preconceived notions about colleges in general or about individual colleges. You need to be open to valid information from wherever it comes. You need to be organized. (Appendices A, B and C will help you keep track of important college planning goals.) You need to consult with people who know you and who know colleges. It's a big decision and while you should direct the total effort, you should also heed the advice of those who are assisting you.

MYTHS ABOUT CHOOSING A COLLEGE

For some reason, the college admission process seems to be a breeding ground for inaccurate perceptions and faulty statements. Students and families often hear comments that are made with the best intentions but which often totally lack any basis in fact. Here are ten myths about the college selection process:

1. *"Colleges are either good or bad."* Nonsense. By what criterion is a college good or bad? In whose eyes is a college good or bad? Academic quality is not easily assessed and, while it is true that some colleges are better known than others, it is not true that a small few are good and the rest are bad. The key question is *not*, "Is X a good college?" Rather, the question is, "Is X a good college *for me*?" Look for colleges appropriate to your educational background, your ability and your personality.

2. *"Future employers and graduate schools give an edge to those who have degrees from prestigious universities."* Not necessarily. As the general level of quality in colleges has risen over the last several decades, and as more and more colleges have distinguished themselves, employers and graduate school admission staffs can no longer rely on the name of the college as the most important selection factor. What *is* important is your success in college. As a result, wise students are matching themselves to colleges within which they have the potential to make good grades and contribute positively to campus life. Such students, with distinguished records in college, are highly sought by company recruiters, graduate schools and professional schools.

3. *"Colleges always choose the 'best' students."* Nope, it's not true. College admission staffs work long and hard to choose students, but no fool-proof or magic formula exists. Their decisions are human and, hence, open to interpretation and judgment. Admission directors often say that in any given year, if they had to go back and make their decisions all over again with the same candidate pool, they would often choose different students to receive letters of admission. So students should be certain their final college list is well balanced in terms of admission difficulty. (In other words, students should apply to some colleges where their admission chances are so-so, and some colleges where their chances are quite good.)

4. *"Schools that cost more are of higher quality."* Why would this be true? A college education is expensive even at a state university. That one college costs double or triple what another school costs says a lot about the size of its state subsidies and its endowment, very little about quality, and nothing about whether the college fits you! Many factors go into determining the fee structure of colleges. Students should look at how well a school matches their own college selection criteria (see Chapter 3) and make few judgments about quality on the basis of cost. If you find a college that offers the right environment for you and costs a bit less, hooray! You are a good researcher of colleges.

5. *"The more rigorous the admission standards, the higher the quality of education."* This relationship is tenuous at best. There are many

reasons a college might have high admission standards. State universities commonly feel an obligation to in-state students and thus out-of-state admission may be quite restricted. A college may have been mentioned in a national magazine, so applications—and admission requirements—have increased as a result. Some colleges describe their mission and their requirements so well that few apply who are not appropriate for that college; hence, while they may accept a high percentage of students, they maintain a very high level of admission competitiveness. More to the point, however, is the fact that quality of education is often not directly related to admission standards. Many superior colleges do not have particularly difficult admission requirements.

6. *"Cost is really important in determining where I can go to college, so I will likely have to attend a local school."* Again, not necessarily. Millions of dollars are given to students and families annually to help defray—or in some cases completely pay for—a college education. The federal government, the states, individual colleges and thousands of public and private organizations make funds available to college students. Again, research is the important strategy. Investigate colleges carefully and use the resources mentioned at the end of the book to help you and your family search for either lower priced colleges or those where you're likely to receive money to help lower the cost of your education. Don't give up before you've even begun!

7. *"Test scores are the most important criterion in college admission."* Not true. Colleges, now more than ever, are using a wide variety of criteria in choosing students and these are discussed in Chapter 7. The quality of the courses you've taken in high school and your grades in those courses are the most important. In addition, your extracurricular activities and your responses to college essays are important. Interviews, while not as important as they once were in the selection process, are still utilized at some colleges. Also significant are any special qualities you might bring to a college campus. Decisions are never made on the basis of only one element like test scores; rather, decisions are made using many different factors.

8. *"There is only one perfect college for me."* Perfect colleges rarely exist. All colleges have good and bad points and all vary in terms of their attractiveness for any individual student. Your goal is not necessarily to find the perfect college; rather, your goal is to research and find those several colleges that best meet your needs.

9. *"I'm a failure if I don't get into College X."* It's hard to convince students that this is not an appropriate way to think or to deal with the process of finding a college. There are many reasons why students are not accepted at a particular college. Your academic record may not be as strong as those of other applicants. Or College X may be looking for a particular set of traits in its applicants and you do not—through any fault of your own—have those particular traits. The college may, for example,

be seeking tuba players or a student from a rural background. The reasons for your denial from College X are unimportant. What matters is that you are at a college where you can use your talents, be challenged in class and have a successful experience. If you plan well, you will have such choices.

10. *"Some secret strategy can get me admitted to college."* No way. No strategy—secret or open—automatically unlocks the admission door. Students who seek letters of recommendation from a Senator or the head of a major corporation (who typically don't know the student) or join clubs in which they have no real interest are trying to strategize. Students have been known to agonize for days over an application essay without realizing it's not the topic that matters, but the content. Students should be themselves as they seek admittance to college. Don't try to "package" yourself in wrappings that are not you. Avoid gimmicks. Trying to gain admission through strategic maneuvering or Machiavellian plotting often results in a major backfire. You might be seen as a phony! Choose colleges that fit; not colleges where you feel your fate depends on sophisticated application strategies.

BEGINNING TO DREAM

Start the college selection process with a sense of freedom. Open yourself up to the excitement and the opportunities ahead. Explore colleges in an atmosphere unblocked by preconceptions or myths.

Dream of the future—your success in college and your success in life. Discard the shackles of negativism. Don't think: "I haven't done that well in high school," "I'm not going to have many college choices," "My test scores are going to prevent my getting into college," "I'm not as good a student as my sister," "I'm never going to live up to my parents' expectations." Instead, think about the possibilities you will have by carefully examining yourself and your goals and by thoroughly exploring which college options are right for you. This attitude will lead to success not only in choosing a college, but in meeting your other lifetime aspirations.

The college experience will require you to exercise your whole being. You will be called upon to think critically and creatively, to be original, to make relationships among new ideas and concepts. Dream of what you can become academically and about the personal and professional value of your new learnings and insights. But college is more than just academics, it's the time for growth in other areas. Dream of cultivating leadership skills, enhancing communication skills, and developing a greater sense of others and yourself. Dream of acquiring practical skills like living on a budget, managing time and lessening stress. Dream about career options so you will feel better about your ultimate career choice. These dreams are the foundation of a successful college experience!

Your first step in transferring your dreams of a successful college experience into reality is picking a college that possesses the right combination of ingredients. The next chapter is designed to start you on that road. Choosing a college will take work, thought and contemplation. But it will be an important lesson in decision-making and reality testing. The right college is where your dreams can begin to unfold.

Chapter 2
Knowing Yourself

Yes, you start the process of choosing a college with a careful look at yourself, not with a list of colleges. For it is your own assessment of your interests, your attitudes, and your abilities that is central to finding a college. Why? Because the purpose of college-hunting is to find the right match between you and your eventual college choice. Many students want to start their search by looking at specific colleges. This sounds good, perhaps, but it is a faulty strategy. Before you start poring over viewbooks and catalogs from colleges, you want to examine yourself as a person and as a student. Such an appraisal will yield data about yourself that will allow you to move with confidence and greater knowledge to the next stages of finding a college.

THE FOUR WORKSHEETS

The four worksheets in this chapter provide an important beginning to that search. The process begins with *Worksheet 1—Self-Survey for the College Bound*. Worksheet 1 contains 80 items designed to assess self-awareness which, ultimately, will help you select the colleges to which you will apply. Complete Worksheet 1 when you have a few minutes; not when you are rushed.

When you finish the Self-Survey, complete *Worksheet 2—Scoring and Interpreting Your Survey*. The scoring is easy; your interpretation will be more time consuming, but worth the effort because it will help you make connections between your responses on the Self-Survey and your potential college choices.

Next, complete *Worksheet 3—Your Activities/Experiences Record*. This worksheet allows you to list significant involvements inside and outside of school. It will not only help you remember your activities and accomplishments (and, therefore, become your "brag sheet"), but it will also become handy when you start to prepare your college applications. Be sure to list anything and everything you have done after the eighth grade.

Finally, move to *Worksheet 4—Your Admission Profile*. This worksheet will give you the chance to see your strengths as a college applicant and enable you to judge realistically how you compare with other candidates for admission.

WORKSHEET 1—SELF-SURVEY FOR THE COLLEGE BOUND

Respond carefully to these questions about your educational attitudes, goals and perspectives. Be truthful and genuine. Keep in mind, there are absolutely no "correct" responses. For each item, check the appropriate answer category—"very true," "sometimes true," "not sure" or "not true." Even if you are unsure of an answer, or your response falls somewhere between two categories, check only one answer per question. Answer each question.

Item	Very True	Some-times True	Not Sure	Not True
1. There are several "causes" in society about which I care deeply.				
2. I often participate in class discussions.				
3. I enjoy reading.				
4. I feel I know myself pretty well.				
5. I'm excited for my college years to begin.				
6. There are at least three things I can do better than others around me and at least three things others can do better.				
7. If I don't understand something in class, I feel comfortable asking my teacher a question.				
8. School is fun.				
9. I normally get excited about the classes I am taking.				
10. I can identify one school subject or topic about which I am truly passionate.				
11. I believe one of the most important reasons to go to college is to get a job.				

Item	Very True	Some-times True	Not Sure	Not True
12. I want to organize myself so I have time for both homework and for out-of-class activities.				
13. If I felt I was really learning something in a class, the grade I received would not matter.				
14. If I want to do something on a Saturday afternoon, I usually don't need my friends to do it with me.				
15. I am satisfied with my listening skills in my classes.				
16. I can truly say I enjoy school.				
17. I will enjoy college a lot more if I can see how my classes apply to real life.				
18. I am interested in and feel comfortable talking about current events.				
19. Going to college is a lot more than the "thing to do."				
20. I enjoy learning things on my own (and not just for a class).				
21. I enjoy hearing and discussing other students' ideas in class.				
22. I see college more as a time for preparing for a career than for discovering my intellectual interests.				
23. A college with a blend of studying and socializing is important to me (even if I'd need to sacrifice my grades a little bit).				

Item	Very True	Some-times True	Not Sure	Not True
24. Even if my friends weren't there, I would still like school.				
25. My friends and I enjoy discussing intellectual ideas.				
26. My parents don't have to remind me to study or do my homework.				
27. My English teachers commend me on the quality of my papers and written assignments.				
28. Making others happy is one of my primary goals.				
29. Most of the time, I feel others understand me.				
30. On most homework assignments, I do everything that needs to be done.				
31. I am comfortable making some decisions without my parents' input.				
32. I want to be able to contribute to society someday.				
33. Unless I have decided on a career, it will be hard to choose a college.				
34. I look forward to school.				
35. I enjoy cultural institutions such as the art museum and the symphony.				
36. I keep my own schedule of appointments.				

Item	Very True	Some-times True	Not Sure	Not True
37. There is more to college than going to class and doing homework.				
38. I often verbalize my feelings about current school or national issues.				
39. I usually find class discussions stimulating and interesting.				
40. Learning about many different academic subjects is really interesting to me.				
41. I usually plan my own social activities.				
42. Unless I know I can use the material I am learning in class, I lose interest quickly.				
43. By late summer, I'm eager to go back to school.				
44. The philosophy "work hard/play hard" appeals to me.				
45. I see many benefits in going to college.				
46. If given the opportunity, I would enjoy participating in a political campaign.				
47. I seldom get "tongue-tied" when trying to express myself.				
48. Taking lots of different subjects in college (English, math, history, etc.) is not as appealing to me as focusing on those subjects I like.				

Item	Very True	Some-times True	Not Sure	Not True
49. I usually go beyond the requirements of a class, not because I have to, but because I am interested in the class.				
50. I like colleges that emphasize pre-professional programs (pre-med, pre-law, pre-business, etc.).				
51. I want to go to college as much as my parents want me to go.				
52. It is easy for me to identify my favorite class in school.				
53. When I know the answer to a question in class, I routinely raise my hand.				
54. I do not feel pushed into going to college.				
55. I am not afraid to take a position with which others will disagree.				
56. One of my top goals is to develop a philosophy of life.				
57. One of the prime reasons to go to college is to meet people who will be influential in my life.				
58. I like a challenge, but I don't want to be academically overwhelmed in college.				
59. It is easy for me to tell people why I want to go to college.				
60. I like teachers who encourage me to think about relationships among subjects.				

Item	Very True	Some-times True	Not Sure	Not True
61. I am ready to begin thinking about my future and planning for college.				
62. I would not be willing to give up my extracurricular interests to make excellent grades.				
63. Learning by discussion is more fun than learning by listening to a teacher lecture.				
64. I read the news and editorial sections of the newspaper most every day.				
65. It is not that important for me to look and act like my friends.				
66. When I walk into a class, I feel prepared and ready to share what I know.				
67. Thinking about one of my weaknesses is not uncomfortable for me.				
68. The thought of college doesn't particularly scare me.				
69. I'm pretty good at making decisions.				
70. Writing essays and papers is relatively easy for me.				
71. Building good relationships with teachers is important to me.				
72. I am willing to study hard in college, but I also want time to be involved in activities and have time with my friends.				

Item	Very True	Some- times True	Not Sure	Not True
73. As far as intelligence, I want the other kids at my college to be similar to me.				
74. I can easily identify the special qualities my friends like about me.				
75. If asked, I could list two or three adjectives that describe me.				
76. I like speaking in front of others.				
77. I believe I know how to motivate myself in school.				
78. I am comfortable with my reading speed and comprehension.				
79. I seldom get homesick when I'm away from home for a few days.				
80. I enjoy volunteering my time to help people in need.				

WORKSHEET 2—SCORING AND INTERPRETING YOUR SURVEY

Scoring your answers is easy if you follow these steps:

1. Go back to the first page of your Self-Survey. Above the words "Very True" write a 9. Above the words "Sometimes True" write a 6. Above the words "Not Sure" write a 3. Above the words "Not True" write a 0.
2. Each of the questions you answered corresponds to an overall theme relating to you as a person or to you as a potential college student. The categories are listed below. For each of your questions, enter your score in the appropriate blank space. For example, start with the category called "School Enthusiasm." Notice that the first item in that category is item number 8. By looking at your answer, you will enter one number: 9, 6, 3 or 0. Go through and fill in all of the blanks below.
3. Total your score in each category. Each score may range from 0 to 72. You can interpret your score as high, medium or low as follows:

   High Scores—57 or above
   Medium Scores—48 to 56
   Low Scores—47 or less

4. For each category check the term "high," "medium" or "low" on the basis of the numbers above.

School Enthusiasm	Participant Learner
8. _____	2. _____
9. _____	7. _____
16. _____	21. _____
24. _____	39. _____
30. _____	53. _____
34. _____	63. _____
43. _____	66. _____
52. _____	71. _____
Total_____	Total_____

My School Enthusiasm score is:

High___ Medium___ Low___

My Participant Learner score is:

High___ Medium___ Low___

Affection for Knowledge

10. ____
13. ____
20. ____
25. ____
35. ____
40. ____
49. ____
60. ____

Total ____

Communication Skills

3. ____
15. ____
27. ____
38. ____
47. ____
70. ____
76. ____
78. ____

Total ____

My Affection for Knowledge score is:

High ___ Medium ___ Low ___

My Communication Skills score is:

High ___ Medium ___ Low ___

Independence

14. ____
26. ____
31. ____
36. ____
41. ____
55. ____
65. ____
79. ____

Total ____

Career Orientation

11. ____
17. ____
22. ____
33. ____
42. ____
48. ____
50. ____
57. ____

Total ____

My Independence score is:

High ___ Medium ___ Low ___

My Career Orientation score is:

High ___ Medium ___ Low ___

Social Consciousness	**Self-Understanding**
1. ____	4. ____
18. ____	6. ____
28. ____	29. ____
32. ____	67. ____
46. ____	69. ____
56. ____	74. ____
64. ____	75. ____
80. ____	77. ____
Total ____	Total ____

My Social Consciousness score is: *My Self-Understanding score is:*

High___ Medium___ Low___   High___ Medium___ Low___

Academic/Social Balance	**Eagerness for College**
12. ____	5. ____
23. ____	19. ____
37. ____	45. ____
44. ____	51. ____
58. ____	54. ____
62. ____	59. ____
72. ____	61. ____
73. ____	68. ____
Total ____	Total ____

My Academic/Social Balance   *My Eagerness for College score is:*
score is:

High___ Medium___ Low___   High___ Medium___ Low___

WHAT DO THE CATEGORIES MEAN?

What does each of the categories mean? What follows is a description of each of the categories. Read through them so that you understand what each stands for and, therefore, what your responses may say about you.

School Enthusiasm

High scorers feel comfortable with the tasks and central qualities of school. In general, they like going to classes and have positive feelings about the academic nature of school. If you scored low here, you may enjoy some of the social features of school more than you like the actual classes, teachers, and classroom information. Additionally, you may not have found school to be a successful academic experience, and your struggle with school may affect your attitude toward it. Your school attitude may impact your feelings about planning for college, your willingness to enter a challenging college environment, the level of competitiveness you prefer, as well as your motivation to stay in school. On the other hand, you may not have enjoyed high school because the particular characteristics of your school may not have been right for you. If that is the case, you have a chance to choose carefully the college you will attend. Your analysis of factors important in selecting a college (Chapter 3) will be particularly meaningful.

Participant Learner

If you scored high here, you want to take an active, rather than a passive, approach to learning. You are not comfortable merely taking notes and regurgitating the teacher's lectures. You want to get involved. You normally do the homework your teachers assign, not only because you have to, but because it helps you learn. You participate in class discussion, enjoy it, and learn from your peers. You read the textbooks and might even read an extra book about a topic in which you are interested. Learning and understanding are so important to you that you are assertive in asking questions of teachers and fellow students. High scorers will likely be most comfortable in colleges where professors are readily available and where lecture classes of 500 are not the norm. High scorers will want opportunities for discussions and seminars as part of their college experiences. In other words, high scorers should seriously consider smaller colleges. Low scorers are interested in and committed to learning, but may prefer to learn quietly and deliberately; low scorers do not need to participate verbally in class to learn course material. Course lectures, reading and out-of-class assignments are normally sufficient ways of learning for the low scorer. Class size will not be as significant a factor for the low scorer as for the high scorer. Low scorers are better able to tolerate large classes. Hence, large sized colleges may meet your needs.

Affection for Knowledge

If you scored high here, the life of the mind is exciting to you. You likely read widely about a variety of topics; you enjoy learning for the sake of learning, not because you may get a good grade. You enjoy talking about ideas, philosophies and trading new perspectives. High scorers will look for academic challenges and colleges that will stimulate their minds. High scorers may even look for those non-traditional colleges that do not provide grades, but only written evaluations of student performance. Low scorers are less comfortable with intellectual ideas and concepts. You may not have yet been exposed to topics, issues or ideas that are compelling. You may not have had experiences that have excited you about learning. You may want to use college as a place to try classes or subjects with which you are unfamiliar; you may be pleasantly surprised by how interesting a new subject might be.

Communication Skills

High scorers here are comfortable with the skills particularly valuable to success in college—writing, reading and speaking. They will usually find college to be a bit less demanding because they are secure with the strength of three important academic skills. Low scorers may want to work to develop more communicative confidence. They may want to exercise care and judgment when selecting English classes in college and may want to seek opportunities where they can best develop their communication skills. They may also want to guard against taking too many classes with heavy reading requirements during freshman year. And they may want to look at colleges that provide extra help with English papers and other assignments.

Independence

Taking charge of one's own life is assessed here. College students choose their own class schedules, their own social "do's and don'ts" and their own hours. High scorers will be comfortable with such freedom. They are less apt to act in irresponsible ways while away from home and, further, are less in need of their friends' approval before making important decisions. They will have little difficulty at colleges where there is a great deal of freedom in choosing classes and in setting your own dormitory rules. Because of your self-sufficiency, you may not need the "excitement" of a college in a large city since you will be able to generate activities for yourself even at an isolated college locale. Low or medium scorers may need more structure to be most comfortable. You may feel more at home with a series of required classes; you may prefer a college with a range of planned activities and things to do. A low scorer may need to work on self-discipline or practice assuming responsibility for decisions and their consequences.

Career Orientation

High scorers see college as a means to an end; in other words, they look at college as a way to get to other lifetime goals—often, to positions of professional competence and lifetime status. They look at college as a vehicle for vocational preparation. As such, they will want to explore professionally related majors and seek colleges where you will be able to keep "on track" toward meeting the needs of your chosen career. A low score here suggests you are very open to the wide variety and extent of learning experiences that college may bring. You may see college as a time for experimenting with and testing a variety of ideas and career paths. The ambiguity of thinking about a range of career choices is not necessarily uncomfortable for you. You may want to explore traditional liberal arts colleges with many options in the humanities, social sciences and sciences.

Social Consciousness

High scores suggest you care about the world and may not be satisfied with the "status quo." Your concern about the state of the world may influence your life and you may need to find outlets for your compassion and empathy. High scorers may want to look for colleges with political action committees, volunteer opportunities or other activities geared to reaching out beyond the bounds of the campus. Some colleges place an explicit value on recognizing one's responsibility to the world. Low or medium scorers may simply not be sensitive to or aware of the numerous opportunities for social responsibility. You are more comfortable pursuing your individual goals.

Self-Understanding

As a high scorer, you are in touch with both good and bad qualities in yourself. You are fairly comfortable with who you are and don't let others tell you who you are. You are accepting of yourself. Your self-awareness will aid you in adjusting to college and in making decisions once you enroll. You will be less prone to behave in college so as to impress others. You are comfortable with your abilities and personality and such comfort will enable you to make mature decisions in college. Low or medium scorers may be just beginning to know themselves. Normally, teenagers' perceptions of themselves are heavily influenced by peers, but low scorers here may be overly responsive to the wishes and demands others have for them. You may be trying so hard to please, you don't know what you really want. A low scorer might find it easier to acquire self-understanding and confidence at a smaller, more supportive college than at an enormous university. Low scorers might look for schools where they'll be a big fish in a small pond.

Academic/Social Balance

High scores suggest you place priority on both academics and extracurricular experiences and you will want to choose a college where you will have a balanced life; that is, where you will have time for both your academic pursuits as well as extracurricular activities and personal time. You should consider colleges within which you are very likely to be similar academically to the majority of other students. You should consider your college choices carefully—being certain you are not getting in "over your head." You will want to choose a college where you are as likely as anyone else to understand the material in your classes, to spend about the same amount of time studying and to be able to have a life outside of the classroom. In researching of colleges, look carefully at the characteristics of students who enroll—what were their grade point averages? test scores? Have they taken courses in high school fairly similar to the ones you have chosen? A lower score here might indicate you place a higher priority on either academics or on social experiences. If you place high priority on academics alone, you may be comfortable at a college where most of your time will have to be devoted to academic pursuits. You may feel comfortable if most of your peers are stronger students than you. If you value social experiences highly, you will want to choose colleges where you are more likely to achieve easily—or where you are better prepared academically than the other students.

Eagerness for College

High scorers anticipate college in a favorable way and are looking forward to the collegiate experience. Adjustment will likely be easy as your enthusiasm will be a great asset in learning to master college life. While you may have some concerns about college, in general your attitude is positive. Because you have played a primary role in deciding to attend college, you likely have specific goals in mind as to the appropriate use of your college years. Low scorers may want to think carefully about their motivations for attending college. Similarly, they will want to give special consideration to the ways they might make college a satisfying and productive experience. Some fears about college, leaving home and being independent are perfectly normal, so if you scored low, involve yourself in the planning and decision-making processes and you will feel more in control and less like you are being pushed into college. But do think carefully about, and seek assistance with, the timing and the nature of your college years.

WHAT DO MY SCORES TELL ME ABOUT CHOOSING A COLLEGE?

Good work. You have now scored each of the categories and learned what each means. Look back on the categories where your scores are highest, where your scores are lowest and where your scores are in the middle range.

All of your scores may have fallen in the high range; or, they all may have fallen in the low range. Either is perfectly normal. Another possibility is that most of your scores fell in the medium range. Again, that's OK. If they fell in the medium range, go back and review the descriptions of each category and decide which facets of the descriptions are true of you. Remember, high scores are not necessarily "good," low scores are not necessarily "bad." Scores are meaningful only in helping you learn more about yourself. Such insight will help you make better college choices.

The following questions pertain to your scores in all of the categories. The questions will allow you to analyze, clarify and understand what your scores mean as you begin the task of choosing your college.

1. List below the three categories in which you received the highest scores:

   Highest score category _____

   Second highest score category _____

   Third highest score category _____

2. In your own words, describe what your *highest* score category says about you.

   _____

   _____

   _____

   _____

3. In your own words, describe what your *second* highest score category says about you.

   _____

   _____

   _____

   _____

4. List below the two categories in which you received the lowest scores:

   Lowest score category _____

   Second lowest score category _____

5. In your own words, describe what your *lowest* score category says about you.

_____

_____

_____

6. Do your responses on this worksheet tell you anything about the type of collegiate environment which would be right for you? Think about the following:
   A. Look at your score in the categories "School Enthusiasm" and "Eagerness for College." What do they tell you about your motivation for going to college?

_____

_____

_____

   B. Look at your score in the category "Communication Skills." What does your score indicate about your writing, reading and speaking skills? How do you assess the academic skills you will need to be successful in college?

_____

_____

_____

   C. Look at your scores in the categories "Affection for Knowledge" and "Career Orientation." What might they suggest about your desire for a general ("liberal arts") education versus one geared toward career preparation?

_____

_____

D. Look at your scores in the categories "Affection for Knowledge" and "Academic/Social Balance." From these scores, determine how much pressure is right for you in choosing a college. While it may be tempting to say, "Oh, in college I'll change and really book it!" Seldom is such a change seen overnight. So be realistic.

_____

_____

_____

_____

E. Look at your scores in the categories "Independence" and "Self-Understanding." What do your scores tell you about your ability to handle the independent living demanded in college? What issues, if any, will you need to deal with prior to leaving for college?

_____

_____

_____

_____

F. Look at your score in the category "Self-Understanding." How well do you feel you know yourself? Don't be distressed if your answer is "not real well." The teenage years, after all, are times of change and you may still be thinking about and working on the many dimensions of yourself. This type of work and thought is commendable.

_____

_____

_____

_____

G. Look at your score in the category "Participant Learner." What does it indicate in terms of size of the college which would enable you to make good grades? What type of relationship with professors will be best for you?

_____

_____

_____

_____

H. Look at your score in the category "Social Consciousness." What might it say about your desire to make a difference in the world?

_____

_____

_____

_____

I. Look at *all* of your scores. What have you learned about yourself which might be helpful in assessing your strengths and weaknesses as a potential college student? What else did you learn about yourself that may help you in "fitting in" to a college?

_____

_____

_____

_____

_____

WORKSHEET 3—YOUR ACTIVITIES/EXPERIENCES RECORD

I. List your in-school and out-of-school activities. Examples: student government, drama, publications, clubs. List them *in order of their importance to you.*

Name of Activity	School Years Involved				Hours Per Week	Weeks Per Year	Position(s) Held
	9	10	11	12			

(list others on a separate sheet)

II. Creative work, hobbies, interests, or anything else not listed above to which you have devoted substantial time.

_____

_____

_____

_____

III. Travel. Describe where and when you have traveled in the last three years.

_____

_____

_____

_____

_____

IV. Academic Honors. Describe any scholastic distinctions or honors you have won, grades 9-12. List the grade level for each. Examples: Honor Roll—11, 12; Certificate in French—10.

_____

_____

_____

_____

_____

V. Other honors or distinctions (athletic, literary, musical, artistic, or other).

_____

_____

_____

_____

_____

VI. Employment

Nature of Work (clerk, delivery, etc.)	Employer (name of company)	Dates of Employment	Approximate Weekly Hours

VII. Description of summer activities. How have you spent the last two summers?

Last Summer _____

_____

_____

_____

Previous Summer _____

_____

_____

_____

WORKSHEET 4—YOUR ADMISSION PROFILE

This worksheet will help you assess your strengths as a college applicant. It lists qualities admission committees feel are important as they review applications, which in turn can give you an idea as to how you might compare with other applicants. Some questions are factual and others are subjective. For either type of question, your straightforward responses and your best judgment will allow you to evaluate yourself realistically as a candidate for admission.

Note: in sections I through VII, the very strongest, most attractive (to the colleges) preparation is marked with (①), the next strongest is marked with (②), the next strongest with (③).

I. Coursework. Check the number of years of coursework (grades 9-12) you will have completed upon graduation for each subject listed. In other words, project years (classes) through four years of high school by making one check per subject.

A. English
_____ 4 years (includes at least 2 in writing) ①
_____ 4 years (less than 2 years in writing) ①
_____ 3 or 3 1/2 years ②
_____ 2 or 2 1/2 years ③

B. Mathematics (College-prep track only—algebra, geometry, trigonometry, math analysis, pre-calculus, calculus)
_____ 4 years ①
_____ 3 or 3 1/2 years ②
_____ 2 or 2 1/2 years ②
_____ 1 or 1 1/2 years ③

C. Foreign Language (remember, for grades 9 through 12 only)
_____ 4 years ①
_____ 3 or 3 1/2 years ①
_____ 2 or 2 1/2 years ②
_____ 1 or 1 1/2 years ③
_____ 0 ③

D. Social Science
_____ 4 years ①
_____ 3 or 3 1/2 years ②
_____ 2 or 2 1/2 years ②
_____ 1 or 1 1/2 years ③

E. Science

_____ 4 years (includes 2 lab courses) ①

_____ 4 years (less than 2 lab courses) ②

_____ 3 or 3 1/2 years ②

_____ 2 or 2 1/2 years ②

_____ 1 or 1 1/2 years ③

F. Have you taken a year of art or music?

_____ Yes ①

_____ No ②

G. Number of subjects in which you will take an Advanced Placement examination.

_____ 5 or more ①

_____ 4 ②

_____ 3 ②

_____ 1-2 ②

_____ 0 ③

II. Class Rank. Check where you rank in relation to the other students in your graduating class. If your school does not rank students, make an educated guess.

_____ Top 3% ①

_____ Top 10% ①

_____ Top 33% ②

_____ Top 50% ②

_____ Lower 50% ③

III. Test Scores to Date. Check score on either or both tests.

Combined SAT I Score	ACT Composite
_____ 1360 or above ①	_____ 32 or above ①
_____ 1300-1350 ①	_____ 28-31 ①
_____ 1130-1290 ②	_____ 24-27 ②
_____ 1020-1120 ②	_____ 20-23 ②
_____ 1010 or below ③	_____ 19 or below ③

IV. Extracurricular Activities. Review Worksheet 3, Your Activities/Experiences Record. Check the statement that *best* describes the extent of your involvements.

_____ Extensive record of involvement in activities and/or individual talent of an extraordinary nature. Recognition extends beyond the local school or community and/or perceived as one of the most outstanding persons in the school or the community. ①

_____ Intensive leadership demonstrated in a major school or community activity (editor-in-chief of newspaper, president of student council, etc.) and/or individual talent recognized as superior. Substantial recognition for achievements. ①

_____ Significant leadership positions or a major participant in school or community activities and/or one or two very fine individual talents. Appropriate recognition for achievements. ②

_____ Some leadership positions or memberships in several clubs or community activities or a significant individual talent. ②

_____ Few in- or out-of-school involvements. ③

V. Basic Academic Tools. In assessing these basic tools, you may feel better about some, not so good about others. Compared with other students, check the one item that seems most true of your note-taking abilities, writing, and reading speed and comprehension:

_____ Excellent note-taking ability. Read with speed and comprehension. Write with clarity and substance. ①

_____ Fine note-taking ability. My reading and writing skills are quite good. ①

_____ Good note-taking abilities. My reading and writing skills are average. ②

_____ So-so note-taking abilities. My reading and writing skills are a bit below average. ②

_____ I often have difficulty taking notes in class and with reading and writing assignments. ③

VI. Study Skills and Time Management. In assessing your study skills, you may feel better about some, not so good about others. Check the one item that seems most true of you.

_____ I complete all assignments on time. Excellent priority-setting abilities. Almost never feel pressured. I know what I want to do with my time and I do what I set out to do. Not easily distracted. ①

_____ I complete assignments on time. Very good priority-setting abilities. Seldom feel pressured. I do what I set out to do with my time. Infrequently distracted. ①

_____ I complete most assignments on time. Good priority-setting abilities. Most of the time, I don't feel pressured. Typically, I do what I set out to do with my time. Seldom distracted. ②

_____ Some assignments completed on time, some late. Average priority-setting abilities. I feel pressured a lot. Not much time planning, but I manage to stay on top of my work. Occasional cramming for tests. ②

_____ Frequently late in completing assignments. Often cram for tests. Usually feel pressed for time. Little or no planning ahead. ③

VII. Academic Recommendations. Check the one set of words and phrases most likely to appear in your teacher recommendations:

_____ "best student I've ever taught," "unbelievably curious," "a real scholar," "Here are specific examples of academic/intellectual depth . . ." ①

_____ "one of my best students in class," "loves learning," "sees relationships between concepts other students miss . . ." ①

_____ "a good deal of intellectual potential," "tries awfully hard," "I see evidence of academic prowess." ②

_____ "Personally, he/she is a good kid," "likable," "completes work on time," "an above average student," "lots of potential for growth." More description of personal—rather than academic—qualities. ③

VIII. Rank Ordering of Admission Strengths. Rank each of the following qualities as they apply to you as a college applicant. For example, if you feel your "test scores" are your strongest feature as viewed by colleges, mark that item with a one (1).

_____ Coursework (strong, competitive courses)

_____ Grades

_____ Academic recommendations

_____ Rank in class

_____ Extracurricular activities

_____ Test scores

_____ Personal attributes/personality

_____ Work experiences

_____ Other. What? _____

IX. Summarize Your Admission Profile below. Look back at your responses to items I through VIII. Comment on your strengths and weaknesses as a college applicant. In how many areas (I-VIII) do you show the very strongest preparation (strongest is indicated with ①)? What about weaker areas? Can you do anything now to strengthen your preparation?

_____

_____

_____

_____

_____

_____

_____

_____

What have you learned about yourself as a candidate for admission? How do you assess your readiness for college? What strengths about yourself will you want to emphasize in the admission process? What weaknesses will you need to take into consideration?

Next, share your responses on Worksheets 2 and 4 with your parents, your college counselor and/or a good friend. How do they react? Do they have any additions or comments about any of your answers? Make notes of their comments and additions on the worksheets. Your counselor will help you to analyze what your responses to these worksheets say about your college choices. Regularly update Worksheet 3 with any new activities, work experiences or awards.

Sometimes learning about yourself can be painful because your sense of yourself may not be what you wish it were or hope it will become. You may have found you are not as strong a college applicant as you thought you were. But keep in mind the essential message of Chapter 1—there are many colleges from which to choose, and your happiness and your comfort in *the* right educational environment is what is most important. In life, each of us deals with the reality of our situation and with the knowledge of our strengths and weaknesses. As you progress through the admission process, keep your strengths in mind but also let your weaknesses serve as a source of direction for improvement. It is not what you are today that is the most important—it is what you will become after your undergraduate years that is most meaningful to a fulfilling professional career and a happy life.

Using the knowledge you have gained about yourself in this chapter, you can now identify the qualities that will make a college a good match for you. That is the purpose of Chapter 3.

Chapter 3
What Are You Looking For In A College?

Of all the chapters in the book, this one is perhaps the most important. Here, you will discover those qualities or characteristics that will make a particular college a good fit or match for you. Chapter 2 was about you. It allowed you to assess yourself on a number of traits which are pertinent to your college planning. Now, armed with that information, you are asked to learn a bit about some of the characteristics of colleges that make them special. Once you have named and identified your preferences, you will be able, in Chapter 4, to list colleges that are right for you.

When you finish this chapter, you will have an answer to the question: What am I looking for in a college? Don't expect the answer to strike you like a bolt of lightning. Rather, you'll have to consider carefully a number of qualities found in colleges and universities: size, location, admission difficulty, academic offerings, and so forth. Each is explained in terms of how it might affect your college experience. So, as you read about each characteristic, think about yourself and your preferences. If, for example, you have trouble identifying your own preferences for size of college, after reading about that characteristic, reflect on yourself and your school experiences so far. What is the size of your high school? Have you felt comfortable there? Have you ever attended a smaller or larger school? How did that feel?

The key to using this chapter well is to have the courage to answer the questions honestly and thoroughly. Do not permit your prejudices about the large state university near you to affect your preferences. Neither should you respond as you think your parents or your friends want you to respond. Answer for yourself. Most of the time, students know what they prefer and where they will do well.

Maybe you are wondering why these college qualities are even important since you simply want the "best" college you can get into. But, wait a minute! "Best" means what is ideal for you, not what is best in some generic sense. The right approach to finding a college is to identify the characteristics that fit you and will make for four successful, happy and productive years. Yes, it will be time consuming to think about all the qualities presented in this chapter, but such an analysis will yield better college options. Regardless of the college you select, you will know *why* you have selected that particular school, and knowing why you have made a choice is perhaps one of the most important skills you can develop. Also, remember, that what is "best" for one student may not be "best" for another student. The only way to determine the "best" college for you is by thinking about all the different features found in colleges as described in this chapter.

As you progress through this chapter, remember there are no easy answers or correct responses to questions about the right size college for you, the right location, or the right academic environment. You might be successful in a range of college sizes, locations, and academic environments. But in some environments you might thrive as a student, while, in others, you might find barriers to your success. Completing Worksheet 5 will help you build your ideal college profile. Pinpointing these qualities, in turn, will lead you to a list of colleges that are right for you.

Proceed methodically through the worksheet. Allow an hour or so for the task. First, read the description of each quality carefully. Then think about how that quality relates to you as a person and as a potential college student. Finally, complete the questions asked of you about each quality.

After you have finished Worksheet 5, proceed to Worksheet 6. Worksheet 6 is a summary of the characteristics you are looking for in a college. Completing it will give you an overview of college features that will lead to your academic and social success.

In Chapter 4, you will identify, then compare, the colleges that meet your now established criteria.

WORKSHEET 5—QUALITIES THAT WILL MAKE A COLLEGE RIGHT FOR YOU

When you see numbers from 1 to 5 sandwiched between two statements, circle the number which best reflects your level of preference. Circle 1 if you have a strong preference for the quality listed on the left. Circle 5 if you have a strong preference for the quality listed on the right. Use 2, 3 or 4 to reflect varying levels of preference.

Quality 1—Size

Colleges vary in size from under 50 to over 60,000 students. Think carefully about which size is best for you both academically and socially. The following considerations may help you:

Smaller colleges provide students with many benefits. First, classes are often more intimate than those at large universities, which allows for greater interaction between student and professor. You'll have more opportunities to contribute in class and it's likely you'll really know your professors. By knowing your professors, you can benefit from their expertise and they can help you with any academic weak points. Further, they will be able to write you knowledgeable recommendations for jobs or graduate schools later on. Smaller colleges are best if you prefer discussion classes (where you are a participant) as opposed to lecture classes (where the teacher does most of the talking). You are also more likely to be able to register for the classes you desire. In addition, smaller colleges tend to place greater emphasis on the personal development of students than do large schools. In other words, it's easier for students to learn about themselves: their personal interests, abilities, and possible career paths. At smaller colleges, teaching is usually the top priority of faculty members—research may be less important. This emphasis may mean more exciting classroom experiences (which often result in increased understanding and higher grades). Socially, smaller colleges provide greater opportunities to participate in extracurricular activities because you don't have to be a superstar to get involved. At smaller colleges, you will experience less competition for the use of academic facilities such as library resources and computers. Also, you usually experience a great sense of community. Because it is difficult to get "lost" in small colleges, they are often conducive to the development of student confidence. Don't discount the advantages of being a significant fish in a small pond—it can do wonders for your self-esteem and sense of accomplishment.

Larger colleges also present students with many benefits. You will notice great range and variety in the courses offered at large schools. You may be able to explore (and perhaps take classes in) two different fields of study -- for example, arts and sciences and engineering. Also, students who are very undecided about the subjects they want to study may feel that large universities (with strengths in many different majors) will be the safest educational choice. Special advanced facilities and resources like state-of-the-art microscopes (and maybe even gas chromotography mass spectrometers!) are available at many large universities. At large universities, students invariably find more activities from which to choose. Significantly, nationally known and popular sports teams tend to be at large universities. Invariably, the publicity for these teams increases a school's name recognition. Further, many students prefer the anonymity a large school offers.

Size considerations often cause students to limit the field of potential colleges too early in the process of choosing a college. Students who would reject larger colleges should remember that some larger universities are more personal than others. Some large universities provide personal attention, such as individual academic advisors. Students from large high schools often say they don't want to attend a college smaller than their high school. Others feel they will miss a certain "collegiate lifestyle" if they attend a smaller college. Remember, smaller colleges can be just as diverse and just as "fun" as larger ones. Also remember, over 80% of private colleges in the U.S.—and almost a quarter of the public colleges—have enrollments of under 2,500. So don't limit yourself too much on the basis of false assumptions about size.

High need for accessible teachers	1	2	3	4	5	Low need for accessible teachers

Smaller classes best	1	2	3	4	5	Larger classes best
Strong academic and career advising are important to me	1	2	3	4	5	Average academic and career advising is fine for me
Many leadership opportunities available	1	2	3	4	5	Few leadership opportunities available
A personal atmosphere is important to me	1	2	3	4	5	A personal atmosphere is relatively unimportant to me

First, look at the following arbitrary size distinctions:

Small size—under 3,000 students

Medium size—between 3,000 and 10,000 students

Large size—between 10,000 and 20,000 students

Largest size—over 20,000 students

Second, on the basis of the discussion and your circled responses above, check those sizes that you feel are best for you:

_____Small _____ Medium _____ Large _____ Largest

Quality 2—Academic Offerings

This category refers to your potential college major and not your potential career. It's important for you to keep that distinction in mind. A major is a subject you enjoy and would like to study in college. A career is what you have chosen as a lifelong field of work. Think about what you would like to study in college. Refer to Appendix D for a list of major fields of study. Do you enjoy English or history? Does psychology or speech communication sound interesting?

Notice the continuum below between "liberal arts and sciences would be best" and "pre-professional training would be best." Liberal arts and sciences is the term used to describe the most general and the most common form of undergraduate education in the U.S. It includes the humanities (English, languages, philosophy, music, art, etc.), the social sciences (psychology, history, political science, etc.) and the "hard" sciences (biology, mathematics, geology, etc.). The liberal arts and sciences often serve as a springboard for future study (for example, graduate school, law school, medical school or business school) and for the world of work. If you are uncertain as to a career, then liberal arts and sciences should be selected below. Pre-professional training (in such fields as engineering, business, education and architecture) often prepares you for a career immediately after receiving your undergraduate degree.

It is perfectly OK not to know what your ultimate career will be. Most high school students do not know. In fact, coming to the wrong conclusion too early about a career is worse than not knowing. Most high school students have not been exposed to many career alternatives, making a final career decision premature. The undergraduate years can be a time of discovery about yourself and your career goals. If, however, you feel confident in your selection of a career goal and want a college that offers your particular program, enter the name of your program below.

Liberal arts and sciences would be best	1	2	3	4	5	Pre-professional training would be best

Exposure to many academic courses	1	2	3	4	5	More career directed courses

What subjects might I consider as possible college majors? (As you research colleges, you may want to look for these among the list of majors in Appendix D.) If you have a career goal, enter it here also:

_____

_____

_____

_____

Quality 3—Coeducation Or Single Sex

This consideration is predominantly for women, although there are some outstanding all-male colleges as well. Don't be too hasty here. Both women's and men's colleges offer special educational advantages and ought to be considered very carefully. For example, several studies have found that students at women's colleges become more academically involved in classes, are more likely to pursue advanced degrees, and show more intellectual self-esteem when compared with their counterparts in coeducational institutions. Further, a women's college gives women more opportunities for academic success in an environment where they don't need to compete with men for both classroom time and positions of campus leadership. Women's colleges are just as fun, just as interesting, and, in many ways, can be just as "real world" as coed schools.

What kind of school would you *consider?*

____ Coed ____ Men ____ Women

Quality 4—Religious/ Ethnic Orientation

Many colleges are affiliated with a specific religious denomination. In addition, some have an historic tie to, or openness toward, a particular ethnic group. Consider the relative desirability of a student body in which most of the students belong to your particular religious denomination or ethnic group. Are these factors important to you in selecting a college?

Insofar as religious orientation, the extent of spiritual influence varies. Some colleges are related to a particular denomination, but are not governed or influenced by the church; these schools tend to have very little religious influence. On the other hand, some have far closer relationships that extend to the required religion classes and/or religious practices (such as chapel services). Regardless of extent of religious life, you might just desire a college where many, if not most, of the students belong to your religion.

Hispanic, American Indian, Asian and African-American students benefit in many ways by attending a college with a high number of students who belong to the same ethnic group. For example, for the African-American student, predominantly black colleges offer students the opportunity to interact with black role models, to develop a "network" of contacts that can be helpful in getting jobs, and to learn in an environment that is relatively free of racial discord. Many respected leaders in government, education and the professions are graduates of these institutions. Similarly, students who might feel isolated on predominantly "white" campuses often benefit from the camraderie and closeness that is possible by being with others who may share their heritage.

Would the presence of other students who represent your faith or heritage foster your sense of belonging? Would you feel like an outcast if you were one of only a few students representing your denomination or ethnic background?

Religious life emphasized	1	2	3	4	5	No emphasis on religious life
It's important that I attend a college where there are many students who share my religious/ ethnic/racial heritage	1	2	3	4	5	It's unimportant that I attend a college where there are many students who share my heritage.

Quality 5—Qualities Found In The Student Body

You will likely find a wide variety of students at practically all colleges. Even so, identifying some of the characteristics about students with whom you would feel most at home can be meaningful as you contemplate your college choices.

Think about the potentially important character traits of the students attending your college. Below, you will see a list of words and phrases that describes students. Look the list over carefully.

First, circle any quality that describes the types of students with whom you would enjoy going to school. In the blanks provided, list any other characteristics you would like to find in your future classmates.

adventurous	down-to-earth	involved	social
aggressive	laid-back	dress conscious	scholarly
spirited	ambitious	energetic	liberal
spontaneous	athletic	friendly	motivated
supportive	career-oriented	fun	open
tightly-knit	caring	idealistic	outdoorsy
tolerant	creative	independent	politically aware
unconventional	conservative	innovative	religious
understanding	cosmopolitan	respectful	diverse
interest in cultural activities			

_____ _____ _____ _____

Second, if you circled more than 5 qualities, go back and check the 5 *most* important ones.

Quality 6—Academic Environment

Academic environment includes academic/social emphasis, academic pressure, and other academic qualities. In this category, you should comment on the relative weight you desire to give to your intellectual development in college. Naturally, since college is an academic undertaking, classes and other "academic things" make up the bulk of your collegiate experience. Yet finding the appropriate level of academic challenge is important to your choice of colleges. Think about how much academic challenge is right for you. Do you want a college where you must work hard and study hard, or would you prefer one where you could earn respectable grades without knocking yourself out? Now, be honest here. Think carefully about how much time you want to spend on academic pursuits in college. If you truly enjoy talking about ideas and intellectual subjects, you may desire a more "academic" atmosphere in your college choice. Also, think here about your response to academic pressure and to competition from others. Are you at home with a tremendous workload? Do you prioritize well? Can you discipline yourself? If your answers to these questions are "yes," you should select a vigorous academic environment. If, however, you prefer to perform consistently at the top of your class, if it's unthinkable for you to get a grade lower than a B, or if you don't work well under stress, you may respond better in a college with normal academic pressure.

In addition to offering certain concentrated areas of potential study (majors), colleges vary in terms of other academic qualities. Would you like close teacher-student interaction? Will you need tutoring help or extra assistance academically? Would you enjoy more freedom or more structure insofar as courses you are required to take? Would work experiences or the availability of independent study enhance your academic success? Would you like a particularly strong study-abroad experience? Is an ROTC program important? If any of these is important, note it below.

Academic vs. Social Emphasis

Very intellectual/ scholarly emphasis	1	2	3	4	5	Balance between intellectual/social sides of campus life

Academic Pressure

Ready/Able to handle the most vigorous academic environment	1	2	3	4	5	Ready/Able to handle normal academic pressure

Other Academic/Curricular Qualities

Circle any of the following which you would like in your college:

close student-faculty interaction	independent study options
tutors/extra assistance available	Army, Navy or Air Force officer training (ROTC)
many study-abroad options	considerable freedom in choosing courses
learning disabilities program	

Quality 7—Activities Available

You may desire a normal variety of activities or you may be looking for a college that offers some specific activity. Would you like to participate in sports? Which ones? At the varsity, club or intramural level? Do you want a college which has many spectator sports? Would you like the option of joining a fraternity or sorority? Are you looking for theater or art or music involvements? Are there any other types of clubs or organizations you would enjoy joining? Refer to Appendix E for a listing of potential college activities. List any activities of interest below.

What activities should the college offer?

_____

_____

_____

_____

Quality 8—Cost/Availability of Financial Aid

Costs vary greatly from one college to another. Many students, however, make too many assumptions about costs too early in the process of choosing a college. There are many forms of financial assistance available. While most of the aid available is given (naturally) to those who can demonstrate need (by the results of a standardized financial aid analysis using forms such as the Free Application for Federal Student Aid), monies are also available for students who have achieved academic excellence or those with special abilities. Below, indicate the extent to which cost/availability of aid is a consideration in your choice of a college. You will want to talk this over with your family.

Cost is a major factor in choosing a college	1	2	3	4	5	Cost is a minor factor

A complete search of financial aid options is necessary	1	2	3	4	5	No search of financial aid options is necessary

Quality 9—Admission Difficulty

Consider what you learned about yourself in Chapter 2. Being realistic is very important here. Consider the level of difficulty of your courses, your curiosity, independence and organization. Review the results of Your Admission Profile, Worksheet 4. Also think about how you compare with others in your own high school graduating class. What level of admission difficulty do you feel you fit into?

The most selective colleges are appropriate for me	1	2	3	4	5	Less selective colleges are appropriate for me

Quality 10—Need For Academic/Social Recognition

To what extent do you desire to achieve outstanding grades and be recognized for achievement outside of the classroom? We all have a need for some recognition, yet individual students vary in their desire for a college where they may achieve these types of successes.

I have a strong need to get good grades	1	2	3	4	5	I have an average need to get good grades
I have a strong need to be recognized for accomplishments outside of class	1	2	3	4	5	I have a low need to be recognized for accomplishments outside of class

Quality 11—Location

The first task here is to decide the relative weight of location in your college selection. Is location more important than other qualities such as overall quality of the college, its academic offerings, size or cost? Or is location relatively low on your college-choosing priority list? Do you want to attend school close to home? Will you want to come home often (even the least homesick come home occasionally)?

Location is the most important factor in choosing a college	1	2	3	4	5	Other factors are more important in choosing a college
I'd like a college close to home	1	2	3	4	5	Closeness to home is not particularly important to me

Think about the following in regard to the location of your college:

Regions of the country where you would prefer to go to college

Are some parts of the country more appealing than others? Give thought as well to the importance you or your parents might attach to the ease and expense of traveling to the college. Do you have relatives or close friends in

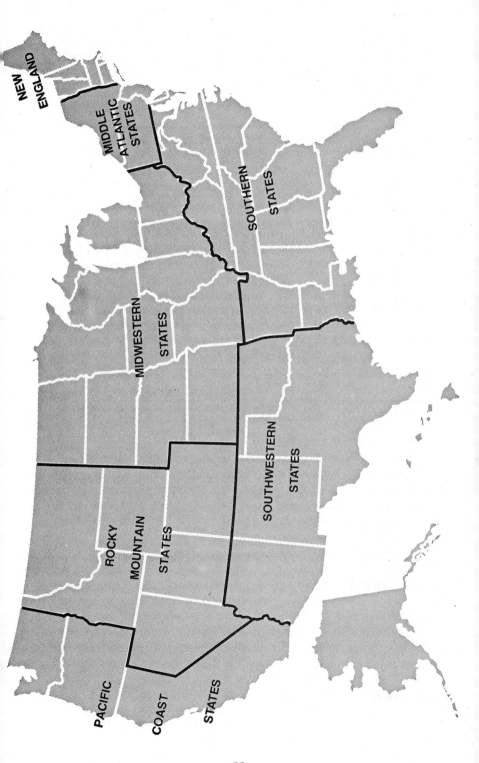

NEW ENGLAND

MIDDLE ATLANTIC STATES

SOUTHERN STATES

MIDWESTERN STATES

SOUTHWESTERN STATES

ROCKY MOUNTAIN STATES

PACIFIC COAST STATES

particular states that you would like to be near? (A relative or friend can be a valuable support system when you're away from home for the first time.) Do you prefer certain types of climates? Do, however, keep in mind that you're choosing an academic environment where you will spend four years—you are not choosing a vacation site! First, look carefully at the map on the preceding page.

Circle those regions of the country you will consider in choosing a college:

Pacific Coast	Southwestern	Rocky Mountain
New England	Middle Atlantic	Southern
Midwestern		

Specific states in which you would prefer to go to college
Indicate any states you particularly like. Try not to think of particular colleges within a given state, but rather, of states you would enjoy.

_____

_____

_____

_____

Close to a city?
Naturally, being in or very near a medium or large city would allow you to take advantage of a number of amenities. If you enjoy cultural institutions such as art museums, the symphony and the ballet, a city or suburban college may best satisfy your needs. Will you go crazy if you don't have at least one large shopping mall and several movie theaters within a half hour of your dorm? Then an urban or suburban college will be best. If, however, you prefer a more serene or relaxed college atmosphere, you may be able to study better in a tranquil location such as a rural college in a small college town. Such colleges may be one or two hours or more from a medium to large city. Typically, college towns show great support for college students and their activities. Store owners may call you by name and cash your check without identification. Most of the services (like pizza places, dry cleaners, etc.) in small towns cater to students. Furthermore, colleges farther away from a city tend to go to great lengths to bring concerts, speakers, and other programs to the campus. Think about the kind of place in which you will be comfortable.

I'd like a college in   1   2   3   4   5   I'd like a college in a
or near a major city   small town or a rural
                                                     location

Quality 12—Academic Success In College

Look carefully at all the factors (Quality 1 through Quality 11) important to your choice of a college. What *else* could a college provide to help you accomplish your academic goals and do your best? Indicate any additional factors here.

_____

_____

_____

_____

_____

Quality 13—Fitting In/Being Comfortable In College

Again, look carefully at the factors you have said are important in choosing your college. Are there any other qualities the college could provide which would lead to your overall comfort with your college? If you were to visit a college tomorrow, is there anything else you would ask about or look for in addition to those factors you listed? Is campus beauty very important? To what extent is campus safety a concern for you? Do you need special facilities or services such as ramps for access to buildings, a kosher kitchen, or psychological services? List any additional factors below.

_____

_____

_____

_____

_____

_____

WORKSHEET 6—CHARACTERISTICS OF YOUR IDEAL COLLEGE

By completing Worksheet 5, you've considered thirteen qualities or characteristics important to you in selecting a college. In the spaces below, summarize what you have discovered about the qualities you seek and their importance. More specifically, review your responses to each of the thirteen qualities. Select the *eight most important* features of a college and write statements summarizing what you are looking for in a college. The examples will help you.

EXAMPLE:

1. I'm looking for a small college because I seek contact with professors and opportunities to get involved in lots of athletic activities. Size of the college is very important to me.

2. I would prefer a college with many Catholic students.

3. All locations are OK but my preference is for colleges in New England.

4. I'm looking for a liberal arts and sciences college.

5. It is very important for me to have a balance between academics and social life. I don't want a pressure-cooker college!

6. I think I should pay particular attention to colleges which either cost less or where I might be eligible for some type of scholarship.

1. _____

_____

_____

2. _____

_____

_____

3. _____

_____

_____

4. _____

_____

_____

5. _____

_____

_____

6. _____

_____

_____

7. _____

_____

_____

8. _____

_____

_____

Chapter 4
Identifying and Comparing Your College Choices

Now that you've learned a bit about yourself (Chapter 2) and identified the qualities that will make a college right for you (Chapter 3), the next step is to find out which colleges best meet your background and talents as well as those that come closest to matching the combination of factors you identified as important to your academic and social success. At this point, then, you need to identify and investigate potential college choices. The goal is to understand the variety of colleges available to you so you can make good decisions about (1) those you will consider, (2) those to which you will apply and (3) the one you will attend.

This might all sound a bit overwhelming; after all, you have some 3,000 colleges from which to make your choices. You may be thinking, "How will I ever find those that are right for me and that I can get into?" You begin by keeping the following three guidelines in mind:

1. *Finding a college requires you to be a good researcher.* Your project is to determine which colleges meet the criteria you listed on Worksheet 6. Don't rely on one single person for information. Molly Jones, from across the street, may not have had a good experience at College A. Does this mean College A is not right for you? No! It means College A was not right for Molly, who was probably looking for a different type of college than you are. So ask lots of people and get many perspectives on colleges you are considering. But remember, everyone seems to have an opinion about colleges—friends, parents, relatives, neighbors and perhaps even your mail carrier! Part of your research goal is to separate valid information from information that is old (colleges do change over time), untrue, distorted, prejudiced, or otherwise misguided. Similarly, don't rely on one single book for all of your information on a particular college. Several books are mentioned below because several sources of information are better than just one. Thus, ask lots of people, read a lot, and stay open to new information. The best advice here is to filter all information and interpret it in a personal manner.

2. *All colleges have good points and bad points.* You have to be ready to deal with both. College A may have the perfect educational program, be the perfect size, be affordable—BUT its location is less than ideal. So, what do you do? You're not looking for the perfect college (remember,

it probably doesn't exist). Rather, you're looking for a list of several colleges where you will be successful. You should weigh the good points against the bad points and then, ultimately, decide whether that college belongs on your final college list.

3. *Don't let stereotypes guide your choice of colleges.* Women's colleges do provide excellent social opportunities. Colorado schools are not all on ski slopes. Students in Maine do get through winter without dog sleds (or even snowshoes). A degree from a "prestigious" college is not a prerequisite (or a guarantee) for landing a well-paying job or getting into an excellent graduate school. The "more selective" colleges are not inherently "better." And the list goes on. The important consideration remains, "Where will I fit in and be successful?"

As you begin your search, be wary of out-of-date or questionable sources of college information. Seek people who know what is currently happening on a college campus. Popular magazine articles listing the "Best Colleges" are unreliable because no totally objective criterion exists for rating colleges. Further, only you and your advisors know what is best for you.

The following pages identify sources of college information and ways to make the most of each source.

PEOPLE SOURCES OF INFORMATION

1. *High school counselor.* High school counselors are, for most students, the key resource people in providing information about colleges. You should meet with your counselor as often as your school suggests and your needs dictate. Give your counselor as much information about yourself as necessary to enable him or her to recommend colleges that are right for you. Share your goals for college and your dreams for the future. Show him or her the worksheets you completed in this book. Remember, however, that counselors are busy people, often with many different responsibilities in your school. So be organized when you visit with your counselor—be prepared with questions and issues for discussion.

2. *College representatives.* College admission representatives visit high schools or have programs in various cities designed to answer questions of prospective students. Be prepared to ask questions of this person. What are the college's strongest departments? What role do fraternities/sororities play in the social life of the college? What financial aid options exist? Any issue important to you should be explored. (Don't let titles of the admission representatives scare you off—colleges have lots of fancy-sounding titles!)

3. *Alumni* (graduates of the college). A recent graduate can tell you a great deal about his or her collegiate experience. Ask questions about his or her major, about the effect of the school's location on the campus life,

about the social opportunities and so forth. Ask, "What do students like most about your college?" You can often get the names of recent alums by asking your counselor or by calling the admission office of the college.

4. *Currently enrolled students.* Current students can be helpful as long as they remain objective and as long as they know you. Since their experience is current and unfolding, such students can provide you with great insights. You will want to ask about their experiences—both in class and in terms of extracurricular activities.

5. *Parents.* Your parents may have insights into various colleges. If they attended college, they may have perspectives about their alma mater or even schools in the same geographic location or in the same athletic league. Further, they may have heard comments from friends or relatives which, when combined with other sources of information, can be helpful in choosing your college. On the other hand, some adults will stereotype colleges as "a party school," "a school for grinds," "a preppy place," etc. Listen to their perceptions when offered, but then check the perceptions yourself.

6. *Friends.* Your friends who have either just gone through the college selection process or who are going through the process right now with you can be another source of information. Their own research, their own impressions, their own travels may be useful to you. Hence, stay tuned to the "college grapevine" at your school or among your friends, but with this word of caution—nobody knows your background and your feelings as well as you do; so, listen attentively, but reserve your final judgments about colleges until you have had a chance to investigate for yourself. Remember, one person's ideal college can be another person's collegiate disaster area.

7. *Educational consultants* (sometimes called independent counselors). Educational consultants are professionals trained to assist students in choosing a college. Many thousands of students benefit from their guidance each year. Consultants combine knowledge about colleges (gained, for example, by traveling to dozens of colleges annually) with the time necessary to be able to explore your situation in depth. Consultants come from a wide variety of backgrounds; some are former college admission directors, others are former high school guidance counselors. While the services of a consultant (like any other professional person) are not inexpensive, fees often represent only a small percentage of the cost of four years at a moderately-priced college. To receive a listing of Educational Consultants, contact the Independent Educational Consultants Association, 4085 Chain Bridge Road, Suite 401, Fairfax, VA 22030, 703-591-4850.

PAPER SOURCES OF INFORMATION

1. *Objective guidebooks.* Most college guidebooks on the market are essentially objective; that is, they are unbiased and give readers basic information about colleges. All of them give such information as academic programs available, general requirements for admission, costs of attendance and other information useful in your search. Examples of these guidebooks are the College Board's *College Handbook,* Cass and Birnbaum's *Comparative Guide to American Colleges, Lovejoy's College Guide, Peterson's Guide to Four-Year Colleges, Barron's Profiles of American Colleges,* and Arco's *The Right College.*

2. *Subjective guidebooks.* The subjective guidebooks generally give a few pages of narrative about each college. They are subjective in that, unlike the objective guides, they take certain positions about profiled colleges. For example, such guidebooks may say, "the following are the best departments at this college..." or "students find this school's location extremely appealing." Because these books make such statements, they often make for easy and interesting reading. The important thing to remember about such guidebooks is that they're not speaking for every student at each college; in fact, some students would disagree completely with the description listed for their own college. Indeed, educators or experts on colleges may also disagree—sometimes fervently—with certain descriptions. Further, the books obviously cannot know what is important to you and cannot compare College X vs. College Y *for you.* At the same time, these books can provide good material which you can validate with your counselor or with your own impressions. Three of the more popular titles in this category are *The Fiske Guide to Colleges,* the Yale Daily News' *Insider's Guide to the Colleges* and the Princeton Review's *The Best 306 Colleges.* And there are other types of subjective guidebooks. For example, *The College Finder,* written by the first author of this book, features almost 500 lists of top colleges in such categories as academics, social life, and athletics. Or, for a subjective listing of colleges listed on the basis of quality in almost 40 academic disciplines, consult *Rugg's Recommendations on the Colleges.*

3. *Specialized guidebooks.* There are a wide range of other sorts of guidebooks available that cover topics of possible importance to you and your family. For financial aid information, students might review *Don't Miss Out: The Ambitious Student's Guide to Financial Aid.* African-American students may want to look at Bowman's *America's Black Colleges.* Athletes will find the *National Directory of College Athletics* of value. A number of books provide help selecting colleges with religious connections. For example, *The College Handbook* (mentioned above) carries a complete listing of colleges by religious affiliation; *Consider a Christian College* and *Jewish Life on Campus* are also helpful. Two books focused on college visitations are *The Complete Guide to College Visits* and *How to Get to the College of Your Choice.* Many other special

interest books are available including *The K & W Guide to Colleges for the Learning Disabled, Letting Go: A Parent's Guide to Today's College Experience, The A's and B's of Academic Scholarships,* and *National Directory of College Athletics.* For an extensive listings of majors offered by colleges, the *Index of Majors and Graduate Degrees* is useful. More information about these books and a listing of other books that can be helpful to you is found in the Reference Section at the end of the book.

4. *Material from the college itself.* Colleges distribute a wide variety of informational materials such as viewbooks, catalogues and other brochures. In addition, some colleges place promotional information on the Internet, often through the World Wide Web. If the literature from colleges of interest is not available in your college counseling office, you will want to request it. A sample post card is given in Appendix F. If you would like some specific information about features like the women's volleyball team, scholarships based on academic merit, or the program in pre-medicine, ask for such information when you write. Read through the literature carefully. While it is true that these materials are designed to further your interest in that particular college and, thus, may be somewhat self-serving, it is also true that your systematic reading can be productive. Some questions to ask yourself as you read are: What does each college emphasize about itself? What majors does the college offer? Is it easy to travel to the college? What feeling do you get from reading the material? Does the college seem friendly? impersonal? spirited? stuffy? full of rules and requirements? diverse?

5. *Computerized college searches.* Some high schools have programs that enable you to look for a college through a computer search. You enter the basic facts (such as major, location or size) you feel are relevant in finding a college and the computer program spits out a list of colleges that meet the criteria you have set. While this may be a good first step, it doesn't replace the other techniques described in this chapter. The reason is this: The computer program doesn't know you and, hence, is unable to determine college environments that are appropriate for you. Further, these software packages don't deal well with ambiguity and most students' lists of factors important in choosing a college are highly ambiguous! Computer searches are best if used at the beginning of your exploration for colleges.

6. *Videotapes and laserdiscs.* Some high schools have tape and disc libraries for students to use. These videos are typically prepared by the colleges and can be helpful in your information gathering. In addition, some colleges mass produce videotapes which you can receive—typically free of charge—from the admission office of the college.

Your personal visit to colleges can be another good source of information if used in conjunction with other material-gathering strategies. Issues pertinent to college visits are discussed in Chapter 5.

ARRIVING AT YOUR LIST OF COLLEGES

Now your search begins. First, review Worksheets 5 and 6 to identify the factors you listed as important. You ought to be able to summarize—to a friend or college advisor—the characteristics of your ideal college.

Now, with help from the sources of information described above, identify those colleges that seem to match your list of factors. List the names of those colleges on Worksheet 7. Your list may be as small as 5 or as large as 40 (20 spaces are provided). Whatever the size of the list, this is where your research and comparisons of colleges begin.

WORKSHEET 7—COLLEGES YOU ARE CONSIDERING

Name of College	Name of College
1._____	11._____
2._____	12._____
3._____	13._____
4._____	14._____
5._____	15._____
6._____	16._____
7._____	17._____
8._____	18._____
9._____	19._____
10._____	20._____

COMPARING YOUR COLLEGE CHOICES

Now is your chance to study each of the colleges you listed on Worksheet 7. This is a difficult task, but also an essential one. Learn about each of your colleges using the methods discussed above—talking to your counselor and other people with accurate information and looking at written materials. No doubt, through your research, you will learn some things about specific colleges that will cause you to stop considering them. For instance, at one school, you might find that fraternities and sororities play a much greater role in the social life than you realized or desired; you might feel this is a significant enough disadvantage for you to stop considering the college.

Through this process of elimination, you will be able to refine and reduce your initial list of colleges and move on to Worksheet 8. From your thinking and reading (or, perhaps, after you have discussed colleges with your counselor), try to decide how interested you are in each of your potential college choices. Does one of your choices sound especially well suited for you? If so, put that college in the HIGH INTEREST column on the worksheet. Jot down the features you like most after the name of the college. Does another of your choices sound much less interesting than you originally thought? If so, put that college in the LOW INTEREST column on the worksheet, again listing those qualities or features at the college that seem inappropriate for you. MEDIUM INTEREST colleges have some good features and some not-so-good features and will require still more consideration.

Remember the following as you complete Worksheet 8:

1. Do not get frustrated by the volume of material written about each college. Read each piece calmly, making notes as you go. Don't say, "all the colleges sound the same." Look for differences.

2. No college is good or bad in the abstract. A HIGH INTEREST college is good because it has the features or qualities you want. A LOW INTEREST college is designated such because you can't get excited about it. Your impressions are most important here, not anyone else's. You are not looking for "good colleges"—you are looking for "good colleges for you." Keep in mind that even among your high interest colleges there may be features that are unappealing to you. No college is perfect.

3. As you think about your colleges, talk with your parents. Have them share in the process of investigating colleges and exploring where you may spend four years. Together, discuss your potential college list.

4. Ultimately, you are looking for a college where you will fit in and where you will feel comfortable.

5. At this point, your goal is not to select the one college about which you feel best. Your goal is to begin to differentiate the colleges knowledgeably and narrow your list to those colleges where you will apply for admission.

WORKSHEET 8—REVIEW OF COLLEGE CHOICES

(If you need more space, please use additional sheets of paper)

High Interest Colleges. *Example:* University of the Trees—lots of courses in communication and other areas I'm interested in, smaller classes, excellent location, has sororities and field hockey.

1. _____

_____

2. _____

_____

3. _____

_____

4. _____

_____

5. _____

_____

Medium Interest Colleges. *Example:* University of the Rain Forest—excellent program in communication, students in viewbook look like me, lower cost, but would I like the location? Also, no sororities.

1. _____

_____

2. _____

_____

3. _____

_____

4. _____

_____

5. _____

_____

Low Interest Colleges. *Example:* University of the Sun—near relatives but fewer courses I'm interested in, too big, seems very focused on academics and hard work.

1. _____

_____

2. _____

_____

3. _____

_____

4. _____

_____

5. _____

_____

DECIDING WHERE TO APPLY

Look carefully at your completed Worksheet 8. Study those colleges in the HIGH INTEREST category. These are the colleges to which you will likely apply. Look also at those in the MEDIUM INTEREST category. Do any of these look equally compelling? If so, these may also become schools to which you will apply. Now turn to Worksheet 9 and list the name and location of those colleges in which you have substantial interest. Although eight spaces are given, the number of colleges to which you apply is dependent on many factors and should be discussed with your college advisors. You may not be ready to complete this final list until the early months of your senior year. Study Worksheet 9 and review it with your people sources of information.

As you review Worksheet 9, ask yourself these three questions:

1. Does your list of schools represent a good match of your interests and talents as well as the strengths of the colleges?
2. Do you have some appealing back-up colleges? Having solid back-ups is important. Some students spend a great deal of time deciding on their reach colleges and very little time choosing their back-up schools. Your back-ups are just as important—don't shortchange them!
3. Do you have enough schools that are also "reach" and "competitive"? The next section describes how to examine the level of competitiveness for your college choices.

If the answer to any of these questions is "no," it is time to rethink your college selection criteria and talk with your advisors. If the answers are "yes," congratulations! You are on the road to an appropriate college choice.

WORKSHEET 9—COLLEGES WHERE YOU WILL APPLY FOR ADMISSION

	College Name	Location
1.	_____	_____
2.	_____	_____
3.	_____	_____
4.	_____	_____
5.	_____	_____
6.	_____	_____
7.	_____	_____
8.	_____	_____

CONSIDERING YOUR LIKELIHOOD OF ADMISSION

Your likelihood of admission is based not only on your background, but also on the extent of the competition for places in the freshman class. Think about your colleges in terms of three categories—reach (colleges where your chances of admission are not likely, but still possible), competitive (colleges where the likelihood of your admission is about 50/50), and back-up (colleges where you will likely be admitted). As you do this thinking, be optimistic but also realistic. Look to see that your group of colleges has balance across the levels of admission difficulty.

No fool-proof method exists for identifying your reach, competitive and back-up colleges (as there are so many individual variables), but the following approaches may be helpful.

Objective guidebooks like Lovejoy's and Peterson's indicate the distribution of class ranks of accepted students; specifically, they tell you what percentage of accepted students ranked in the top fifth, second fifth, etc. of their high school classes. This is helpful information against which you can compare yourself. Is your high school class rank on par with the class ranks of the other students at a college of interest? If so, this may be a competitive college for you. Naturally, if your rank is either significantly higher or lower than those you see, the college might either be a back-up (if higher) or a reach (if lower).

Guidebooks such as Barron's and Cass and Birnbaum's list colleges on the basis of "Most Competitive," "Very Selective," etc. While these categories are open to interpretation, they can still provide another perspective. Are all your colleges in the "Highly Competitive" category? If so, perhaps you need to identify a few colleges in a less competitive category. Another consideration is the data some colleges report about the percent of applicants they accept. The average acceptance rate for colleges nationwide is approximately 80%. Hence, if all of the colleges you are considering have acceptance rates of 20%, your likelihood of being one of those accepted applicants is lower, and you may want to add a few schools where your admission chances are higher.

Another strategy is to note the range of SAT I or ACT scores of students accepted at your college choices (these may also be found in the guidebooks). Compare those ranges to your scores. If your scores are similar to the majority of students admitted, that college *might* be a competitive or a back-up. If your SATs are much lower than those of most of the students admitted, that school *might* be a reach. You will learn in Chapter 6, however, that college admission officers take many factors into account to determine your "acceptability"—not just your test scores. Lower test scores can be offset by strong, college preparatory courses. In addition, your grade point average, extracurricular involvements, level of curiosity and so forth may suggest a greater or lesser chance of admission.

Still another method for considering your choices might be to get information about grade point average, difficulty of courses taken, test scores, etc. from the college itself. This is possible when representatives visit your high school, or you might write or call the college and request this data yourself. Armed with this information, you can you can use your answers from Worksheet 4 to assess how your admission profile compares with that of each college you are considering.

Most important in examining the category of each of your choices is a discussion with your college advisor. He or she will use knowledge based on experience with lots of other students to help you make these judgments.

APPLICATION COMPLETION: KEEPING ON TRACK

Next, complete Worksheet 10, The Application Timetable. This timetable will help you get organized and monitor the numerous deadlines associated with applying to college. You should complete Worksheet 10 as follows:

First, complete the left column with the name of each college to which you will apply. This list comes from Worksheet 9. If you are applying to more than eight colleges, make a copy of the timetable. Read the application materials for each college thoroughly. Be aware of procedures applicable to each of your college choices. In addition, find out how your school processes applications. What are your responsibilities? Is your high school responsible for mailing the applications? Are completed teacher recommendations given to you, sent directly to the college or given to the counseling office?

The next step is to fill in the column labeled "reach, competitive or back up." Review the previous section in this chapter and determine to the best of your ability the level of selectivity for each of your college choices. Be certain you have at least one college in each of the three categories, Your counselor will help you with this.

Then, check to see if you have an application for each of your colleges. If you do not, send a postcard requesting materials. A sample postcard is shown in Appendix F. If you have the application, record the deadline for each college. In addition, some colleges allow you to apply through the use of generic, "common" applications and by floppy disk.

Next, you want to establish *your* specific target date for submitting your application. This will keep you organized and moving forward during the fall of your senior year. Look at the application deadlines; clearly, your target date should be prior to the deadline set by the college. Many students try to complete all of their applications by Thanksgiving of their Senior year; others try to have them in the mail by the time of winter vacation. The deadlines set by large state universities may be in the winter or even spring, but your deadline should be earlier in order to maximize your chances of priority consideration.

In the next two columns, record both the number of essays as well as the number of recommendation you need for each college. MAKE A SEPARATE LIST OF ALL OF YOUR ESSAY TOPICS. Remember, the word "essay" as used here includes any writing task given to you by the college— personal statements, short answers or brief paragraphs. With your list of essays you can tell which assignments are most common, whether there are any overlapping topics (in other words, essays you can adapt for more than one college), and, from these considerations, you can systematically start writing. Begin work on your essays well before the due date for the application so as to give yourself time to refine and polish your writing. Knowing how many teacher recommendation you need will help you to follow through and see that your teachers complete their forms in time to meet the application deadline.

When you finish each application, record the date it was mailed in the appropriate column. Remember to make a copy of your completed application and essay(s) before you mail it in case your application gets lost or misplaced along the way.

The final two columns allow you to personalize the Timetable. These columns give you the chance to keep track of anything else of importance to you. You may, for example, use one of the columns to indicate the date you send the required financial aid forms to the college, The columns might also be used to indicate which SAT II: Subject Tests the college requires, or the dates of your campus visit or music audition. Record how you are going to use the columns in the blank spaces on the Timetable.

Having reviewed many ways to identify and compare colleges, the next chapter focuses on an important way to learn about a college: the campus visit.

WORKSHEET 10 — APPLICATION TIMETABLE				
College or University	Reach, Competitive or Backup?	Application Received?	Application Deadline	My Target Date for Completing the Application
1.				
2.				
3.				
4.				
5.				
6.				
7.				
8.				

How Many Essays to Do?	How Many Recom- mendations to Get?	Date Application and Essay Sent	Date Test Scores Sent		

Chapter 5
Learning From Campus Visits

The process of making a good college choice involves several important steps. By considering your goals, your interests, and your achievements, you have begun the process of considering colleges and comparing them to your requirements and ideals.

Chapter 4 presented the variety of resources available to help you make a good college choice. Your parents, college advisors, and a variety of publications will give you some sense of the life at a particular college. But *one* important way for you to know if you might feel comfortable is to visit the college itself and observe your own reactions to the campus, the people, and the general atmosphere of the college. This chapter answers the questions most commonly asked about campus visits.

1. Why should I visit colleges?

The best reason for visiting is to learn about the college first-hand. Usually students return from college visits with new impressions and perspectives about places they know only from written material or the comments of others. A campus visit makes a college come alive. While you may not be able to visit some colleges, visits are an excellent way for you to find out if the college will be a good place for you to live for four years.

So visit to learn more—to help with the fact-finding process. Not many colleges still require an on-campus interview and seldom will an interview turn out to be the critical factor in a decision on your application. Still, visitation can be very helpful in your college shopping. If cost or time are issues, you should use other resources to find out about your potential college choices—at least in the initial phases of your investigation.

2. How should I prepare for campus visits?

Although it sounds obvious, you must first decide which colleges you will visit. While you may have neither time nor resources to visit all the colleges your counselor recommends, neither should you visit only those that are the most competitive for you. In general, you should plan campus visits to four or five schools that represent different levels of competitiveness and choice for you. Chapter 4 discussed ways to think about your chances of admission. Ideally, you should visit your first or second choice schools only after visiting others. You will profit from the experience and the perspective you gain.

3. When should I visit colleges?

The best time to visit colleges involves a number of considerations and will vary for each student.

If you have planned well ahead and have identified colleges appropriate for you, the spring of your junior year is a good time to see campuses.

Many students visit campuses during the summer between their junior and senior years. While this is not the best time to see a campus "in action," (since there may not be students on campus) it's a relaxed time for admission staffs—and, perhaps, the easiest time for families to get away. Often, during the summer, entire families will tour colleges together, combining their vacations with campus visits.

The fall of your senior year is a good time to see the campus, and at some schools the best time to schedule an interview. Some selective colleges fill their entire appointment schedule early, so, the key words for visits to highly selective college campuses are: call early.

The spring of your senior year, after you have received all your admission decisions, is a good time to visit and make your final choice. Unfortunately, admission offices can be quite hectic at this time of year and making travel arrangements without much advanced planning can be expensive.

If you participate in a sport, and you want to continue that sport while in college, you may want to visit campuses while your sport is "in season."

Your other decision is what day of the week to visit. Again, this decision depends on the goals you want to accomplish. If you simply want to see the campus, you can visit anytime. If you want to gain a real sense of campus life—meet some students, sit in on classes and participate in some typical activities—then you should schedule your visits during weekdays of the regular school year. While some admission offices are open on Saturday mornings, most campuses are fairly dead until noon on weekends. Also, to get a good sense of a campus and its people, you want to visit on a "normal" day, so avoid exam weeks and big football game weekends.

Whatever your schedule is like, remember that campus visits will be most beneficial if they occur after you have discussed college options with your counselor and completed your own research on recommended colleges (and completed Worksheet 8 in Chapter 4). Don't just "head West" (or any other direction, for that matter) to visit colleges in a willy-nilly fashion.

4. I am visiting several colleges in one trip. How much time should I spend on each campus?

You should try to spend as much time as possible at each college. An overnight stay is ideal. Most students need at least half a day for each visit; a visit of less than three hours is insufficient for a complete view of a college.

5. What should be done before I visit?

You should arrange for your visit by calling the admission office at each school you plan to visit. Since letters take too long and often result in inconvenient appointments, call several weeks in advance of your desired visit. Be aware that the *most* selective colleges fill up interview times several months ahead, although it is still possible to have a campus tour or a group information session. Group sessions are described in Question 11.

Schedule your appointments so you can arrive on time. Study road maps and transportation schedules; allow extra time to find a college if you are unfamiliar with the region or city in which it is located.

When you call, talk to a staff member of the admission office and tell him or her what you would like to do during your visit—take a tour of the campus, talk to students, attend a class, meet with a professor, eat a meal in a dining hall, and, if at all possible, spend a night in a campus residence hall. Some students will want to meet with a coach, others will want to see the studio art facilities. Your visit depends on your interests. Whatever you do, *talk to students* during your visit. Also pay attention to bulletin boards and the campus newspaper; both are good guides to campus activities.

The admission office will normally be able to make arrangements for a campus tour, visits to classes, and either a personal interview or a group information session (see #11). Often, they will be able to arrange an overnight stay in a residence hall. Sometimes, however, the admission office may ask you to make additional calls to set up appropriate appointments. If you know students on the campus you plan to visit, you may want to call them and ask if you can be their guest for a night.

When you call the school, ask them to send a written confirmation, a parking permit, and a campus map. These will ease your planning. If you do not stay on the campus, ask the admission office for recommendations about motels or hotels nearby.

6. What sort of questions should I ask?

Since the purpose of your college visits is to research your level of comfort at the schools, plan your questions accordingly. Some questions may be general and apply to every school you visit; others may be more specific. You will gain the most insight into the school you visit if your questions go beyond the obvious—the ones answered in the factual publications. Ask questions about those issues and topics that matter to you. To arrive at questions important *to you*, review the characteristics of your ideal college, Worksheet 6. A few general questions follow.

Questions to ask students or admission officers:

- Why do students select this college?
- What is the attitude of students about the college?
- What do students on campus rave about?
- What do students complain about most?
- How active is the social life?
- What type of student seems happiest?
- What are the most popular majors?

- What are the most popular extracurricular activities?
- What are the opportunities for extracurricular participation?
- What are student traditions?
- What types of services exist for personal and career counseling?
- What happens around here on weekends? Do students stay on campus?
- How safe is your campus? How comfortable will I feel walking through your campus alone at night?
- Do students know one or two professors well enough to ask them for a work or a graduate school recommendation?

Questions to ask admission officers or professors:
- What are typical course requirements—exams, papers, etc.?
- Who teaches introductory courses—professors or graduate students?
- What arrangements are made for advising and tutorial help?
- What opportunities exist for independent study and study abroad?
- What departments are considered outstanding, weak, and average?
- After graduation, what do typical graduates do?
- What constitutes a typical freshman-year program?
- Why is this a good college for me to study my selected major?
- What if I am unsure about my major? Is this a good place to explore?

Having asked these questions and others, your visits will be most beneficial if you use Worksheet 11 to make notes about each campus after each visit.

7. Should my parents go with me?
Parents can be very helpful in helping you determine your level of comfort and your ability to succeed at a given college. Also, parents often have questions of their own. They do have an investment—financial and otherwise—in your plans for the future. While parents can be helpful and supportive throughout the visit, they should not participate in the interview. The interview is with you. Perhaps they will want to schedule a visit with a financial aid officer or just walk around the campus while you are involved in an interview. Following your visit, share your reactions and observations with your parents before asking for their impressions. Then weigh their comments with yours as you think about each college.

8. What is a personal interview on campus and how important is it?
The personal interview is rarely a required part of the admission process, and is seldom a deciding factor in accepting or rejecting a candidate. In fact, the interview most often serves to confirm other information about a candidate. Similarly, an interview does not transform an unacceptable applicant into an acceptable one. An interview can, however, be an excellent way to learn about a college. It is a two-way exchange. You should be ready to ask questions that will help you learn more about the college,

and be ready to answer questions that will help the interviewer learn more about you. Some typical questions and requests follow:

- Tell me something about yourself as a student.
- How did you become interested in this college?
- What things are most important to you as you compare colleges?
- What are your interests, strengths, and weaknesses?
- Do you have any questions? (This is often asked. Be ready!)

Do not hesitate to identify one or two things about yourself you want the interviewer to know as the result of talking with you, and be sure to mention them when the interviewer says, "Is there anything else our (admission) committee should know about you?"

In addition, do not hesitate to share the leadership of the interview. You are not on the witness stand; it is seldom a "grilling." You should use the interview as a chance to see if the college fits you, too. Moreover, colleges will want to make both your campus visit and your interview a positive experience for you.

Also, many selective colleges will grant local interviews with alums; these are helpful and alumni/ae can be valuable sources of information about a college. Remember, however, alums are likely to be volunteers, not employees of the university. As such, their level of current information about the college varies considerably.

9. What should I do during the interview?
A few tips follow:

- Dress comfortably. Wear regular school clothing. Do not wear odd or flamboyant clothes—unless that's really you!
- Be honest and be yourself. Do not try to second guess what the interviewer wants to hear.
- Ask questions.
- Make eye contact with the interviewer.
- Make a note of the interviewer's name.
- Try to find out where you stand. Near the end of the meeting, ask the interviewer about your admission chances based on the information you've shared.

10. What happens if I have a bad interview?
If your interview does not go well, *do not* despair. Rarely are admission chances ruined as a result of an awkward or uncomfortable interview. The interview report is only one element in considering an applicant; the total picture of a student is most important.

11. What is a group information session?
If you don't desire a personal interview or you cannot arrange one, be sure to ask if the school offers a group information session. This is exactly as

the name suggests—an admission officer speaks to a group of prospective students and parents, and then often addresses their individual questions.

12. What should I do after the visit?

Send your interviewer a thank-you note. This is a gracious and polite response to a good campus visit and an excellent way to mention something about your interview that particularly impressed you, and that will enable the interviewer to remember you.

13. Do colleges ever have special days when prospective students can visit?

Yes, many colleges schedule special visitation days for prospective students. During a college-day program, a school often focuses all its resources on the needs of visitors. If you enjoy other students and like to participate as a member of a group of students, the college visit program will be an exciting experience. If you want more individual attention, you should schedule an individual visit.

14. My family's funds are limited. We can't afford a tour of colleges. How can I learn about colleges?

In most cases, you don't need to travel thousands of miles to learn about colleges, just visit a few colleges in your state. Choose nearby schools; private, small liberal arts colleges as well as medium or large state universities. These visits will help you get the feel of different types of institutions— then you can visit the schools to which you have been admitted later.

Attend any campus visit programs sponsored by colleges near you. Sit in on a class and, most importantly, talk to students. Talk to currently enrolled college students when they are home on vacation. Attend college night programs at your high school. Visit with college alumni. Or, finally, telephone the admission office and request that a student call you back to talk about the college.

15. How can I tell if a college is a good one for me?

The college visit should not make the decision for you. Keep in mind what you have learned in this book about the characteristics of your ideal college. Measure what you see and hear against the qualities you listed as important on Worksheet 6 in Chapter 3. But a few final tips are in order:

- *Do* record your observations. Use Worksheet 11.
- *Do* talk to students on every campus.
- *Do* follow up your visit with a thank-you note.
- *Do Not* evaluate the school only on the basis of a visit with one student.
- *Do Not* judge a college solely on the basis of your impressions of the tour guide.
- *Do* analyze the whole school.
- *Do* take photographs.

- *Do Not* let the weather on the day of your visit totally influence your impression.
- *Do Not* make snap judgments.
- *Do* judge schools after you return home and have time to think about all of your visits.
- *Do Not* let perceived quality affect you. Your task is to find the right colleges for *you.*
- *Do Not* judge the college *solely* on the basis of impressions made on your visit. Remember what you have read and heard about the college before your visit.

16. How can I remember my impressions of each college?

Write them down! *Campus Visit Notes* are provided on Worksheet 11. You will want to make a copy of the worksheet for each campus you visit.

WORKSHEET 11—CAMPUS VISIT NOTES

Name of College _____

Location _____

Date of Visit _____

Name of Interviewer_____

Campus Facilities:
Comments on how the campus strikes you.

_____

_____

_____

Student Life:
Comments about student life on campus.

_____

_____

_____

Academic Factors:
   Comments about academics.

_____

_____

_____

Overall Impressions:
   What did you like best?

_____

_____

_____

   What did you like least?

_____

_____

_____

Other Facts You Want To Remember About This College:

_____

_____

_____

Overall Assessment Of How Well This College Fits You:

Not Very Well   1   2   3   4   5   Extremely Well

Chapter 6
Making Your Essays Work For You

You have, at this point, already made some important decisions about the colleges you will consider as well as the colleges to which you will apply. Now, you are ready to begin the process of preparing your college essay. The essay is typically the most time-consuming part of the college application, and it deserves the most attention.

This chapter is divided into three major sections. First, you will complete Worksheet 12. Worksheet 12 will explain the reasoning behind the essay questions commonly found on applications and assist you in thinking through your own answers. Second, you will complete Worksheet 13 which presents opportunities to brainstorm additional essay ideas. The third part of the chapter provides some specific hints for writing an excellent and highly communicative essay.

This chapter, however, does *not* include complete essays used by students for their own college applications because such samples may impair your own creativity and constrain your thinking. No essays are generically "good" or "bad" or "right" or "wrong." There are only good or bad essays *for you.* Everyone has his/her own special qualities and stories to tell. And those stories are the substance of good essays.

BEFORE YOU START

First, in case you are wondering, colleges do read the essays students send them. While a few large colleges and universities rely primarily on grade point averages and test scores to make admission decisions, the vast majority of college admission committees actually read, study, and think carefully about the words you write on your applications. In fact, at some colleges, your application will be read by two, three, four or more people. Moreover, your application may be discussed at length by a group of admission people in a committee meeting. The application essay, then, for all practical purposes, should communicate, on paper, what you would like a group of strangers to know about you. Many students are unused to using words and paper as a key way of communicating images of themselves, and this makes applications and essays difficult for many students.

Perhaps the most formidable barrier, however, to essay writing is a lack of confidence about writing in general and personal writing in specific. Many students start the process by wondering what colleges want to see in an essay. This type of thinking is a waste of time! Don't try to "psyche out" an admission committee by deciding what it wants to read. Rather, the most important question you can ask yourself is: What is it about me that I want colleges to know? Colleges are vitally interested in knowing about you, your interests, your feelings, your reactions, your insights, your qualities, your passions, your satisfactions and your disappointments, to name but a few. The extent to which you tell your own meaningful story in an interesting, readable and articulate way is the extent to which your essay is good.

No easy, quick solution is offered here for building writing confidence. But, often, students are surprised to find that the incident or reaction they thought most unsuitable for a college essay is exactly the one that is most important and revealing about them. Do not try to be anyone else in your essay. Tell about yourself and you'll write a wonderful essay! (One note here, too: Sometimes your parents think you are so terrific they want you to tell the colleges how terrific you are. While their intent is admirable, your essay should not seem as if you are patting yourself on the back—save that for someone else!)

In their applications, colleges ask a variety of essay questions. Some questions are very specific (for example, "Describe a significant experience, activity, achievement or person in your life") and others are very broad and general (such as "Tell us something about yourself that will help us get to know you better"). Many colleges call the essay a personal statement, some make the essay optional, and some require no essay at all. With few exceptions, though, most students gain by enclosing an essay or personal statement with their application (even when it is not required). Worksheet 12 lists the most common essay questions with a series of brainstorming strategies for each. By brainstorming, you'll arrive at one or two ideas you can use in preparing your own (yes, your very own) answer to the question.

After you have completed Worksheet 12, move right on to Worksheet 13. Your answers to the open-ended questions in Worksheet 13 may suggest other essay topics to consider as you begin working on your own applications. These two worksheets should give you a head start on your essay writing.

When you have finished this chapter, and after you have identified your college choices, make a list of all the essays, personal statements and other writing assignments for the colleges to which you are applying. Then, prioritize your essay requirements on the basis of application deadlines and your own target dates, as listed in Chapter 4, Worksheet 10. Worksheet 10 will help you keep track of other important steps in completing your college applications.

Topic 1—Discuss a significant experience, event or achievement and its impact on you.

Of all the essay questions asked by colleges, this one is perhaps the most common. It provides you with an amazing number of opportunities to write about those aspects of your life that are most important to you.

The key word in this question is "significant." The word "significant" is critical because it requires personal reflection; an experience, event or achievement becomes significant when it causes us to see ourselves or others in a new or different way. In other words, just because you've never weathered a typhoon or won a national ski racing championship doesn't mean you're wanting for "significant" experiences. Even at seventeen, you've had experiences that have affected you deeply; experiences others will find interesting. For example, one student produced a very thoughtful essay about the changes that occurred at home when her mom decided to go to college full-time. Another student wrote about the significance of visiting his grandmother every summer on a farm in Nebraska. Still another student received a traffic ticket and wrote about his reactions to and learnings from his encounter with the law. Another student completed a very interesting description about the expanded family he gained when his mother remarried.

As you reflect on possible topics, remember, an experience that affects you has no prescribed length. An important experience may last several minutes, several hours, days, or months. The most important consideration is that the experience had a memorable impact on you. In this essay, you will describe the experience and how you felt about it and discuss what it reveals about you. Still having trouble? Then do this: Close your eyes, and for a few minutes go through your memory bank. Think about everything that's happened to you since you became a high school freshman. No doubt a few of those memories are a bit more vivid, a bit more clear than others. Normally, those vivid memories are or were "significant" experiences.

Now you try. On the lines below, briefly list a few of your significant experiences:

_____

_____

_____

_____

_____

_____

_____

_____

Excellent! Now, in a few phrases, explain why one of those experiences was significant. What did you learn about yourself as the result of the experience? Here's how one student began:

> *My younger brother's struggle with a severe hearing loss has affected me significantly because I have had to grow up rapidly and assume some added responsibilities at home. Sometimes it's real scary, because I don't exactly know how to do the things I am expected to do in taking care of him.*

It's your turn below:

_____

_____

_____

_____

_____

_____

_____

Terrific! You have the beginnings of the essay about a significant experience. If the question directs you to write about a significant achievement or accomplishment, you will do the same kind of thinking.

Topic 2—Discuss an activity (extracurricular, community, family, or work) that has had the most meaning for you and tell why.

This question is relatively easy. Think about everything you do to occupy your time when you are not in school or studying. Refer to Your Activities/Experiences Record, Worksheet 3. Do you play the piano, sew your own clothes, play sports or write articles for the school paper? Do you work at a job, take care of a baby brother, or volunteer at a nursing home? The key here is identifying an activity that has meaning for you.

First, list the meaningful activity:

_____

Now think about the ways in which the activity has been meaningful for you. As you think, go beyond the obvious. It is normal, for instance, that a team sport like soccer might be meaningful because you learned teamwork. But no doubt you also learned a great deal more than teamwork by playing soccer. Did you learn how to deal with disappointment? Did you learn that "people skills" are not as easy as you thought? This is one student's thesis about her experiences as a field hockey player:

Playing field hockey last year was significant for me. I learned that I am not as good a leader as I am a follower, and for the first time, I learned how to deal with people I don't like.

Now, write a sentence that tells, specifically, the way or ways in which the activity you listed above has been meaningful or significant for you.

_____

_____

_____

_____

_____

Great! You've just written the thesis sentence for an essay regarding a meaningful activity. In the Hints Section later in this chapter, you'll find some suggestions on how to develop the sentence above into a complete essay about an important activity.

Topic 3—Discuss your educational and/or your career objectives.

This question stumps many students. Often it is not easy for them to identify or name their plans for the future. But, for just a minute, think about why you want to go to college. Look back at your Self-Survey results (Worksheet 2). What did you learn about yourself as you thought about your answers in such categories as "School Enthusiasm," "Career Orientation" and "Eagerness for College?" Some of your thoughts may become your answer to a question about your educational goals. Again, go beyond the obvious. Many students say they want to go to college to get a job. But think about those things that you want to learn in college that will make you a better employee or employer.

Now list below three reasons why you want to go to college:

a. _____

b. _____

c. _____

Next, think about your personal and professional goals. Do not feel awkward if you have no idea what you want to do when you get older. You may simply want to list the careers you have considered and provide a brief statement explaining why or how you have thought about each field. Maybe friends or family have suggested various career ideas to you and you may have thought seriously about a few of those. Or, ask yourself: If I were paid an excellent salary to do what I like best, regardless of stature or social value, what would I do with my life? Such issues and questions are often a good beginning to career exploration.

Using the space below, write an answer to the question: What are your thoughts or ideas about your career or professional goals?

_____

_____

_____

_____

_____

But what if the question also asks you to list your personal goals? Don't worry; simply think about those aspects of your personal life that college might change or expand. For instance, perhaps you're looking forward to meeting new friends, to becoming more independent, to participating in a sorority or fraternity, to joining a new service organization, to trying an activity or skill you've never done before. All of those can comprise the personal goals you'd like to accomplish in college.

If an essay topic asks for some personal goals, state a few ideas below:

_____

_____

_____

_____

_____

_____

Topic 4—Why have you selected University of the Universe?

Some of the colleges you are considering may ask you why you have selected their particular institution as a school to which you will apply. At this point, all of the good thinking and research you've done in the preceding chapters will really come into good use. Review the factors you listed as important in selecting a college, specifically, Worksheet 6 in Chapter 3. Compare those factors to the distinguishing features of the University of the Universe (UOU). You should find that many features at UOU fit the criteria you feel are important in your college choice. For example, UOU may be perfect because you were seeking a small liberal arts college with friendly students located in a rural area. For this essay, list the qualities that led you to choose that particular college. You might also indicate other factors that promoted your interest. Perhaps you visited UOU or talked to its representative. Or you may have been impressed with what alumni said about UOU. All of these may be reasons why you feel UOU is a good choice.

First, list one of your current favorite colleges:

_____

Second, describe why you would like to attend:

_____

_____

_____

_____

Topic 5—Indicate a person who has had a significant influence on you and describe that influence. A similar question: If you could spend an evening with any person, who would it be, why would you choose that person, and what would you talk about?
Again, think back through your memory bank to those persons (friends, family, teachers, coaches, ministers, etc.) who have had an impact on you. Think carefully about the ways in which each of these people has influenced you. How has this person caused you to change? What did this person teach you? What role model or behavioral example did this person set for you? Be specific. Talk about particular examples or instances in which this person displayed for you the influence he/she had. And the most important part of this question: Identify, in precise language, the reasons you have selected the person you chose. It is not enough to say, "I admire my Uncle Sam because he is a kind person." You must connect the quality of kindness to you. Do you admire Uncle Sam's kindness because it is a quality you are trying to emulate yourself? Or do you see the kindness he displays as similar to but different from the kind acts you do? Remember, the point of the essay is to tell the admission committee something about you. You are simply using the impact and qualities of a significant person to tell your story.
First, write the name of a person who has had an influence on your life:

_____

Now, tell about that influence:

_____

_____

_____

91

Topic 6—Tell us something about yourself that might be helpful to our understanding of you. A similar question: In the space provided, tell us about your activities, accomplishments, significant experiences, and/or anything else that might be helpful in understanding your candidacy.

These questions are so broad that answering them completely, yet succinctly, defies the imagination. The key here is to choose some aspect of yourself, your background, your family, your activities, or your accomplishments on which to focus. *Do not* try to tell the committee everything there is to know about you in 300 words! It can't be done, and if you try, it is likely to be a boring recital of every award, contest or honor you ever won. For this response, choose one significant feature, describe it completely and in a compelling fashion, and tell your reader your own reactions or responses. This is the beginning of one student's response to this question:

For as long as I can remember, music has been a part of my life. I even remember the lullabies my mother sang. My early start with music has continued to my teenage years and it has been for me a way of relieving tension as well as providing enjoyment.

This student then went on to tell how, when she practices, she dreams of being on stage at Carnegie Hall. She tells how she felt when she made a mistake in a recital, and she shares the excitement of winning a major music award at a state conference.

By now, it should be very clear that a simple listing of awards and accomplishments does not help your reader learn about you. If your reader is to gain any sense of the person you are, you must write of your reactions and feelings towards those awards, defeats and accomplishments. A list of awards is simply that, a list.

OK, now try yourself. What would you like a college to know about you?

_____

_____

_____

_____

_____

_____

Topic 7—Describe a significant academic experience.

This question is not one of the most common, but it can and does appear on many applications. A significant academic experience can be a particular class you liked. Think about why the class was particularly good. Was it a dynamic teacher? Was the subject material particularly fascinating? Did you like the assignments? And be specific about the ways that class made you think and grow. A significant academic experience can also be a particular book or project in which you became totally absorbed. What made the book or the project or the experiment so exciting to you? Finally, an academic experience can be significant because you really worked hard to understand a topic or a concept and finally mastered it. Here's how one student started:

Chemistry was a significant academic experience because it was the most difficult class I have ever taken. With work, I finally understood the concept of the mole. In chemistry, I learned that science is not just an obscure subject, but rather one that has implications to real life.

In the following space, jot down an idea or two about a significant academic experience:

_____

_____

_____

_____

_____

Another way to answer this question is to consider the extent to which you have lived up to your potential as a high school student. Think about yourself as a student. If you have worked up to your potential, write a brief statement about your strengths as a student. For example, were you successful in high school because of your organizational skills? Your willingness to work hard? Your excellent teachers? If you have not yet worked up to your abilities, why not? There may be perfectly valid reasons—illness, learning difficulties, or changes of high schools. Or was it a lack of motivation, or did you place a priority on your out-of-school activities? If some real barriers have impeded your success, you should feel comfortable talking about them.

Have you lived up to your potential in high school? Why or why not?

_____

_____

_____

_____

_____

Topic 8—Discuss a particular local, national, or international issue. A related question: Discuss a particular piece of literature, music or art that has meaning for you.

These questions are not as dissimilar as they look. The key to your responses is to link them to yourself, your feelings and your experiences. You may be concerned about the environment, but unless you have a personal connection to the topic of recycling, for example, your essay may be little more than an objective (hence not personal) discussion of that topic. The best topic for the "issue" essay is a topic about which you feel so strongly you could write an editorial for your school or city paper. In questions like those above, your reader is most often uninterested in an expository essay; as with all the other topics, you should use the issue or the work of art as a means of telling about you, the topic about whom your readers really want to know. Remember, your readers do not need your summary of *The Great Gatsby*; they do want to know how and why the book affected you.

As practice, use the following space to tell about an issue of concern *or* a piece of art of significance to you:

_____

_____

_____

_____

_____

The eight questions provided in Worksheet 12 commonly appear on college applications; however, as indicated earlier, the possibilities for essay questions are endless. Don't let the questions stump you; remember, the central purpose of the essay, regardless of the specific question, is to let the admission committee get to know you. So, if your applications contain questions not among the eight just discussed, use the following exercises to give you ideas on ways to answer the uncommon question.

Listed below is a series of adjectives. Quickly circle those words you feel are true about you most of the time.

able	determined	independent	original	respectful
accepting	direct	ingenious	overconfident	responsible
active	diplomatic	innovative	passive	retentive
adaptable	disciplined	inspiring	paternal	scientific
aggressive	doer	intelligent	perceptive	self-reliant
ambitious	driver	introverted	perfectionist	sensible
analytical	efficient	intuitive	persuasive	sensitive
articulate	energetic	jovial	playful	sentimental
assertive	enterprising	kind	pleasant	serious
aware	enthusiastic	knowledgeable	powerful	sincere
brave	extroverted	lazy	practical	skillful
calm	fair	leader	precise	sophisticated
carefree	flexible	liberal	principled	sociable
caring	follower	lively	progressive	spontaneous
cheerful	frank	logical	protective	stable
clever	free	loving	proud	strong
competent	friendly	loyal	punctual	supportive
competitive	genial	maternal	questioning	sympathetic
confident	gentle	mature	quiet	tactful
conforming	giving	merry	radical	thoughtful
conscientious	gregarious	modest	rational	tolerant
cooperative	gullible	methodical	realistic	tough
courageous	happy	naive	reasonable	trustworthy
creative	helpful	negative	reassuring	understanding
critical	honest	nervous	reflective	useful
decisive	honorable	objective	relaxed	vulnerable
demanding	humorous	observant	reliable	wise
dependable	idealistic	optimistic	religious	witty
dependent	imaginative	organized	reserved	workaholic

Which three of the circled words describe you the best? List them here.

1. _____

2. _____

3. _____

Now, think about activities, achievements, failures, and/or experiences that might best illustrate these adjectives. For instance, you might feel the word "caring" describes you well. When was that quality particularly evident? Perhaps you might illustrate your caring qualities by describing your feelings and insights the time you helped your friend out of a troublesome situation. Or perhaps you can illustrate caring by talking about the menagerie of stray animals you have collected at home. The point here is important. Do not simply say you exhibit certain qualities; show those qualities to your reader. In other words, when the reader is finished with the essay he or she should be thinking, "What a caring person" without you ever having to mention the word "caring."

Again, it's your turn. First, write one of the three qualities you listed above:

_____

Second, provide a brief illustration of how that quality describes you:

_____

_____

_____

_____

_____

Just one more brainstorming task. Complete the following open-ended sentences:

1. People describe me as . . .

_____

_____

_____

2. During my high school days, I have succeeded at . . .

_____

_____

_____

3. During my high school days, I have failed at . . .

_____

_____

_____

4. The thing most often misunderstood about me is . . .

_____

_____

5. An important decision I made in high school was to . . .

_____

_____

Do any of your answers to the above open-ended questions suggest any other potential essay topics? If so, list them below:

_____

_____

_____

_____

_____

HINTS FOR EXCELLENT ESSAYS

1. Students often feel that negative, disappointing or uncomfortable experiences or events should not be used in essays. Some fear these experiences might reveal a weakness or insecurity and that such information would be a liability for an applicant. Nonsense! A sensitive, but not self-pitying exploration and explanation of a difficult sophomore year or an uncomfortable experience at camp can constitute a wonderful, insightful essay.

2. Write from the heart. The more you can tell your reader how it felt to have a car accident or make an important decision, the more your reader will know about you—and that is the goal of a good college essay.

3. College essay writing follows several of the same basic principles used in your high school English classes:
   - Use an organizational strategy that enables you and your reader (the admission staff at the college) to gain some sense of an organized flow of ideas. Your organizational plan enables your essay to fulfill a purpose, to go someplace; it gives it a logical beginning, middle and end.
   - Write your body paragraphs first. Do not attempt to write your introduction first. Normally, you should decide what it is about you that you want to talk about and then make a few notes or an outline about how you will develop that topic.
   - Write a clear thesis or controlling statement.
   - Make your grammar clear and your spelling correct.
   - Make your examples specific, specific, specific. Your reader wants to know how you lost the close sailboat race, and you will help

bring this to life if you describe how the boat looked and the details of the race day. Your precision should help your reader actually see the boat, the race, and the trophy. Be specific and concrete. Your essay will be interesting to read.

- Finally, a college essay differs in one important way from an essay you might write for an expository writing class. Your college essay should *not* be written in the third person (*"one* should realize. . .") or in the second person ("if *you* are on student council. . ."). Rather, your essay should be written in the first person ("from student council, *I* learned. . ."). When you write, you should tell your reader, "I felt disappointed when I dropped the football," or "I was overjoyed when I earned an A in my very difficult math class."

4. Students often ask how long an essay should be. While requirements and specifications on length vary (and most colleges give clear instructions), most college essays are about 250-500 words. In double-spaced typing, that's about one and one-half or up to two pages. Now, that's not so bad!

5. Perhaps the next most common question about essays is whether or not the English teacher or your parents ought to read your essay. While English teachers can be very helpful in reading for grammatical and spelling errors as well as for some content and development issues, remember that they read as English teachers, not as admission officers, and the difference in perspective is key. Also, when parents read essays, they should not attempt to rephrase or restate your ideas into more complex language. Nor should they discourage you from sharing those reflections about yourself that may strike your parents as revealing a weakness or an insecurity. You are human, as are admission officers, and your human insights are those that make for superior essays.

6. Finally, do not believe the lore that admission committees only read essays that are highly unusual ("a poem is really impressive" or "why don't you write your essay on the back of a photograph of your grandmother?"). If creativity or humor or poetry is you, fine. If not, do what is honestly you. Creative essays or stream of consciousness essays are acceptable if they meet the primary criterion mentioned earlier—that the essay allows the college to learn about your strengths, your motivations, and your sensitivities.

7. Okay. Are you ready? Do you know the essay topic that one of your colleges lists on its application? If you completed Worksheet 10, you have, in front of you, the essay questions to which you must respond. Have you done your brainstorming? Try to formulate a thesis sentence for one of your essays. Remember, write your main points and your body paragraphs first; try writing furiously and without stopping. Try to write at least a page. Do not, at this point, censor your work. Do not stop to correct spelling or look up words in the dictionary. Simply tell your story as if you were writing a letter to a friend. Then, continue

writing furiously until you have completed your story. Add an interesting introductory paragraph that intrigues the reader enough to go on. Add a conclusion and voila! Obviously, you'll next want to read for grammatical and spelling errors, but you have a draft of your essay. Does it communicate? Does it say something interesting about you? Is it written honestly and with feeling? Is it completely you? If so, hooray!

Having written your essays, you may be interested in how essays fit into everything else the college reviews in making a decision on your application. The next chapter explores the dynamics of the admission process.

Chapter 7
The Admission Process Revealed

The process of selecting students is often cloaked in mystery and intrigue. What goes on behind the closed doors of admission offices? What causes one student to be admitted and another to be rejected? Surely there are some secrets which, if known, will help you get admitted. Right? Unfortunately no. What goes on in admission offices is actually not all that mystical.

It is not mystical if we just think of who these people are and what their task really involves. Admission officers (Dean or Director of Admission, Associate or Assistant Directors, Admission Counselors) are professionals whose job it is to recruit and select both the numbers of students and the types of students who will ultimately benefit the college. They are hired to tell the story of the college to potential students and then to select, from the pool of people who pay their application fee and submit their admission application and other documents, those students who are judged most likely to meet the goals of their college. And the goals vary widely. For some colleges, the goal is to admit students who have evidenced tremendous scholarship and who will benefit from the library holdings and the strengths of the faculty. For others, it is to enroll a freshman class large enough to allow the college to continue to expand and add new departments or programs. Most typically, colleges seek to achieve several objectives when selecting the freshman class.

Most important to keep in mind is the fact that college admission officers are human beings with a job to do. They have great sensitivity to individual differences. Hence, discussions about what a college is "looking for" in a student vary tremendously. Evidence of scholarship or curiosity may mean one thing to one admission officer and something entirely different to another admission officer. They want to do the best job they can in meeting the goals set by their college in recruiting and selecting students.

Historically, admission offices existed for the purpose of reading student applications and making accept and reject decisions. During the last ten years, admission offices have focused their efforts more and more on recruiting and attracting students. As a result, competition at selective institutions is more intense than ever. Admission officers who have focused on student recruitment are doing a good job—the pool of applications to their institutions is increasing—thereby enabling them to select the best qualified (in their eyes) for the spaces available in the class.

Sound advice, then, is not to manipulate the admission process with gimmickry, chicanery or hocus-pocus. Such strategizing is likely to fail because colleges are well aware of the difference between genuineness and gamesmanship. Do not try to be different just for the sake of being different. There is no essay topic that always works, no interview technique that guarantees acceptance, no person whose opinion of you (via a letter of recommendation) can always sway admission committees. You may hear that you should write an essay that is creative and "far out" (and possibly even write it on a Kleenex tissue!). You may hear that colleges "love" kids who are involved in Big Sisters or the local shelter or whatever. You may hear that colleges really like those who take Japanese or who enroll in a summer course at a nationally known university. But none of these things is necessarily or always true.

Given that complex strategic maneuvers are of little value, how should you look at the admission process? Here are a few suggestions:

1. *Be yourself.* This may be the most important fact of all when applying to colleges. Tell your story without trying to play the role of a super sophisticate, a super scholar or whatever. Tell your own story and *tell it well.*

2. *Make sure your course load is reflective of your best intellectual efforts.* Be realistic here also. As noted below, colleges do care what classes you have taken and what you contribute to your classes. Take the most advanced classes you can manage without getting in over your head. Senior year is no time to slack off. Admission offices are very positive about a strong college preparatory program, with four or five solid subjects each semester. Colleges will admit you primarily on the basis of your ability to be successful doing college-level work. Show the colleges what you are capable of achieving.

3. *Do something productive with your time.* Be as constructive as you can be in whatever arena fits you. That arena may be creative arts or leadership or community service or work or sports or a hobby—or something else.

4. *Be informed.* Care about people and issues. Care about national or international events or happenings in your city or your school. Learn to articulate your views with reason and even with passion.

Remember the point made throughout this book: You will have good college choices if you carefully seek out those choices. Don't sit and fret because you may not get into Stanford or Swarthmore or Sewanee. If these colleges are right for you, for heaven's sake, explore them and apply if they meet *your* criteria. But if you feel that, realistically, you should not reach for the most competitive colleges, be comfortable with your choices. Many people attend lesser-known undergraduate colleges and eventually become political leaders, corporate executives, skilled doctors, lawyers, and teachers. If you must strategize, do so by finding colleges that, in fact, fit you and that will draw out the best within you.

FACTORS IMPORTANT IN SELECTING STUDENTS

As indicated above, colleges use many factors in selecting students. Not all of those listed here are used by all colleges, but they account for most of the input into the eventual college decision. The precise blend of factors, as stated, varies by college and even by individual members of the admission staff at the same college.

1. *High school program.* The courses a student takes in high school are often, and correctly, viewed as the most important factor in selecting a freshman class. Colleges look to see what you have taken in comparison to other applicants and in comparison to what is offered at your high school. Your Admission Profile (Worksheet 4) gives you an indication of how your program compares with others. College admission officers are sensitive to the extent to which an applicant has pushed himself or herself as reflected in the student's choice of classes. It is important to say again that you should take the most challenging program (filled with honors or Advanced Placement classes and many solids during your senior year) you are able to handle. But, as stated, know your limits as well. You want to balance the academic, extracurricular and personal sides of your life.

2. *Grades and rank-in-class.* Grades provide evidence of your capabilities and motivation. Grades are only significant, however, in light of your courses. Sometimes students ask if it is better to take harder classes and get lower grades or easier classes and get higher grades. Unfortunately, this question has no simple answer. Many of the most competitive colleges state that their applicants have taken the most difficult classes and received A's in them. But the answer depends on you. Surely, you should not balk at taking a more advanced class with the fear you might receive a B. Because colleges weigh these factors carefully, it is up to you to select the right program for you. Rank-in-class gives the colleges another indication of your performance vis-a-vis others at your high school. Of course, high schools vary considerably and ranks depend upon the level of competition at your high school.

3. *Test scores.* Not all colleges view test results in the same way. Some are more "test conscious" than others. A few have even made the submission of test scores optional. By and large, test scores are viewed as important, but not as the critical variable in making an admission decision. Most colleges count high school program difficulty and performance as more important in making decisions on entering freshmen. The three entrance examinations most often used by colleges are: 1) The

Scholastic Assessment Test (SAT I); 2) The American College Test (ACT); and 3) SAT II: Subject Tests. Colleges differ in which of these they require, and students should check application materials carefully for testing information.

4. *Extracurricular activities.* There is no such thing as the "perfect" list of extracurricular activities. Some students have exhibited extensive involvement with leadership in one or two activities. Other students have a broad set of involvements in several activities. At the most competitive colleges, accepted students have quite often achieved recognition that extends far beyond their own high school or even community; students who are recognized by their teachers and sponsors as having "really made a difference." The question often asked in this area is, "what has a young person done with his or her time?" It is up to you to demonstrate, on your application, that your activities have been meaningful and noteworthy. Use Your Activities/Experiences Record, Worksheet 3, to help you think about the strength of your activities. (Worksheet 3 can also be helpful in completing your applications.) Many admission officers would prefer to see a student involved in fewer activities with evidence of sustained commitment than someone who merely joins many clubs and organizations.

5. *Personal qualities.* This factor is hard to define but it certainly plays into the admission decision. Admission officers want to know a prospective freshman as well as possible, and thus, such qualities as depth of intellectual curiosity, sustained interest in or commitment to a local or school issue, altruism, fairness, and particularly meaningful reactions to a life experience or a response to a setback can be, and often are, significant. Some students show dedication to community service, others have special talents or abilities. Still others have travel or work experiences. Any of these may catch the eye of an admission officer. Your level of initiative in day-to-day living can be important, so can an ongoing appreciation for ethical, historical and world issues. Your college essay, the comments of teachers and others who know you, and/or an admission interview can tell the admission officer about such personal qualities.

6. *The application itself and your essays.* Your responses to application questions and, particularly, essay questions give admission officers a sense of what is important to you and how you think. As such, they become a "window to your mind." Essays were discussed in Chapter 6.

7. *Recommendations.* Most colleges require prospective freshmen to ask at least one person to complete a recommendation on his or her behalf. These recommendations are another clue to you as a person and, more importantly, you as a student. As such, students should give careful thought to those who will be asked to complete a recommendation form. Get recommendations from those who know you well and can comment frankly on your intellectual skills as well as your potential.

Frequently, your high school counselor is asked to write a recommendation for you. As such, it is important to get to know your counselor well. Some of the most competitive colleges also ask for teacher recommendations. Don't necessarily select the most popular teacher, the teacher who gave you the highest grade, or the teacher whom your classmates say "writes the best recommendation." Pick teachers who really know you and will take time to write insightful, thoughtful, honest letters. Because your intellectual potential is being evaluated through your recommendations, those from "big wigs" such as Senators, the Governor, a leading professional in your community (who may be a graduate of the college) or other well-known persons rarely are helpful—unless that person has worked with you and can contribute something significant to your admission file. On the other hand, you should not hesitate to ask someone who knows you well—say an employer or the leader of a summer experience—to write a letter to a college on your behalf. These letters have the potential of assisting the admission staff in knowing you. But consider your recommenders carefully. Too many recommenders can be distracting and work against you.

These are the seven factors most commonly considered by admission officers in deciding on new freshmen. But there are others. Motivation is important, as is your ability to overcome adversity. The most selective colleges seek those who are best able, by virtue of their intelligence and maturity, to use the resources—teachers, equipment, libraries, and so on—the college provides. It is important to remember, however, that admission formulae seldom exist. Students and parents often ask, "What test score do I need to be admitted?" or "What grade point average is required for admission?" While it is true that a few (typically, those that are large and state-supported) universities actually do use an admission index that consists of some combination of grades and test scores, most college admission decisions are multi-faceted and, hence, hard to predict. No college ranks every applicant and then accepts a certain percentage of them. If you have completed Your Admission Profile (Worksheet 4) realistically and honestly and have read the section on "Determining Your Likelihood of Admission" in Chapter 4, you should have some sense of how you might compare with other applicants.

BEHIND THE SCENES

Keep in mind, admission officers take all of the factors described above into consideration. Raising your test scores by, say, 100 points, does not mean your chances of getting into a very competitive college suddenly go from fair to good. This is true because your course load, grades, activities, and so on likely have not changed. Furthermore, an outstanding essay will not compensate for a weak program of classes or little evidence of commitment to academics. This is not to suggest that score improvements or spending time on your college essay are unimportant. But keep in mind that colleges consider the full complement of factors as they read applications for admission.

Central to this discussion is the realization that colleges admit students for many different reasons and with different admission portfolios. The most competitive colleges are seeking a diverse and "balanced" class. They seek some students because of their scholastic credentials alone and others because of what they bring to the campus in terms of unique perspectives, skills and interests. One student may be favorably considered primarily because of top grades and several involvements. Another student may be admitted because of musical or athletic talents; some hail from geographic areas underrepresented at that college. Some colleges give special consideration to disadvantaged students because of a commitment to increasing access to higher education. Some colleges respond favorably to sons or daughters of their alumni. Typically, none of these qualities (alumni, geographic diversity, athletic talents, children of university employees, etc.) gets a student admitted, but they figure into the total picture and may tip the scales in favor of a particular student.

As such, it is significant to remember that admission decisions are not, by definition, fair and equitable. Why? Because they are human and, thus, subjective. What may grab the attention of one admission officer may not even raise the brow of another one. How one college elects to balance a class may be different from how another college does it. Further, the relative weight of test scores, essays or extracurricular activities varies widely from one college to the next—even among colleges perceived as similar in their level of admission difficulty.

As an applicant, then, your best game plan is to approach the college choice process realistically. As stated before, you do have choices and you should concentrate on colleges where you will "fit in." "Fitting in" is still more important than "getting in." In terms of "getting in," you should focus on colleges where you perceive you have a reasonable chance of admission. Sure, have one or two "reach" colleges (where your chance of admission is less, but still possible) but spend the majority of your time on those schools where your background and skills suggest a good chance of admission. Don't become unglued because there are a few colleges where you will likely not be admitted. As stated in Chapter 1, be happy because over 2,500 colleges do want you! Success in college is what really counts.

ADMISSION DECISIONS

In closing this chapter, let's talk about the results of all of your work— the actual decisions from the colleges where you have applied. Most likely, your thoroughness led to appropriate college choices, and those choices have now produced acceptance letters from colleges—colleges that really fit and in which you can make a contribution. If so, congratulations are in order. But you may also have been denied admission to a school that really appealed to you. It is tempting to suggest that that college is really not the best fit and your other choices are surely more appropriate. It is also tempting to say that the admission process is sometimes unfair and that good students are often left without an acceptance while others, perceived as less well qualified, have gained admission. Both of these temptations, while perhaps truthful, miss the true feelings that surely are present whenever such a setback hits. Rejection hurts, and it will hurt for awhile and there is no way around it. But reactions to such setbacks distinguish a person with character and grit from someone who is mushy, and dull, a quitter. Your ability to handle a denial with guts says a great deal about you as a person and as a successful college student—wherever you decide to attend.

The next chapter focuses on the important role your parents play in your college decision-making. While it is written for your parents, you should read it as well. It may enable you to see the college planning process from their point of view and provide perspectives on some of the issues you may be talking about at home.

Chapter 8
Parents As Educators in the College Selection Process

The process of identifying, researching, and ultimately selecting a college is one that should involve the entire family, and throughout this book, students have been encouraged to discuss their thinking with their parents. While the rest of this book has been written for the student, this chapter is written for parents. So the *you* in this chapter refers to parents!

Your role as the parent of a student going off to college is a difficult one. There are so many issues, so many emotions, so much contradictory advice to consider. Some parents feel as overwhelmed as their sons and daughters. But, like the student, parents should approach this college-seeking process with systematic persistence. Move, with your child, through the various stages of choosing a college as they are presented in this book. Your role as counselor, advisor, and helper will aid your prospective college student in growing and learning through this process. Students should take the lead throughout this process. They should actively seek your advice and help, but they have to be responsible for the decision about to be made. If a parent takes over the process of choosing, the student doesn't learn. If the parent is excessively anxious, the student will act likewise.

You want your son or daughter to make a good decision, and you have worked hard over the years to enable your young person to attend college. Be clear about your expectations and your goals, but give students the room they need to contemplate the issues they face in choosing a college and in making the right decision. Ron Miller, a faculty member at Lake Forest College in Illinois, makes a good point when he says, "I've been working with this age group for some years now and I've learned they're a lot like flowers: they need nurturing but they also need to be left alone."

Let's begin by discussing seven common questions from parents as they and their students begin to think about college.

Question 1—My daughter can't possibly plan for college. She doesn't even know what she wants to study! Is it important for my daughter to know what she wants to do in life?

While this concern is common and well-intentioned, parents and students must view college planning as a process significantly different from career planning. In the truest sense, the undergraduate years are intended as a time for both self-discovery and intellectual discovery. One of the best ways of selecting an eventual course of study (a major) and/or a career is by identifying those subjects and classes in which a student has interest and by discovering those intellectual and personal talents or gifts that each student possesses. While it is difficult for a high school senior to make the leap from identifying favorite subjects to identifying a career path, let your daughter's likes and dislikes play a role in her initial major selection. But keep in mind, an art major can wind up in medical school and an English literature major can later go to divinity school.

Hence, you will want to set aside (at least for now) any concerns you may have about your daughter's lack of a definitive career direction. If she has no idea about potential careers, she may want to look at colleges that offer a broad range of academic programs (a liberal arts and sciences emphasis) so she can keep open a wide variety of options while making a decision. On the other hand, if she has a sense for what she would like to study, that's great too. Remember, though, the typical college student changes his or her major at least twice during a four-year college program. What is important is that your daughter *actively* explore different career possibilities during her undergraduate years. This is accomplished by taking a wide variety of courses, asking teachers about vocations in their fields, participating in internships, using vacations for work experiences in career areas of interest, and utilizing the resources (such as the career planning office) available on college campuses.

By the way, many colleges ask students to declare a major field on their admission application. If your daughter remains undecided, she should choose a subject of interest without feeling as though she's locking herself into a definitive career path.

Question 2—We want our son to attend a college we have heard of— after all, when he gets out into the "real world," the name of the alma mater can be the ticket to employment. Right?

Not necessarily. This question can be answered on two levels. First, as mentioned in Chapter 1, the United States has approximately 3,000 colleges. Name recognition among colleges varies by area and industry. In other words, a set of parents living in Connecticut employed by the hospitality industry will likely recognize a considerably different set of colleges than will a set of parents who live in New Mexico employed by the aerospace industry. Oh, but you ask, aren't the Ivy League colleges the "best?" Wouldn't any prospective employer give an absolute edge to an Ivy League graduate? No, on both counts. First, a college's membership in the Ivy League Athletic Conference is no guarantee of academic or social fit for any given student; most importantly, though, perceptions among potential employers about any given college are almost as variable as the employers themselves.

Increasingly, as mentioned earlier, employers are interested in knowing what any given student has "done" at his or her college. Academic success is reflected by grades, research, independent study, study abroad, honors, and special projects. Social success is evidenced by leadership, participation, involvement and commitments to activities, people, and projects. In the end, these accomplishments matter far more than the actual name of the school that a student lists on a resume. Significantly, a recent study supported by the U.S. Department of Education found that the name or prestige of the college a student attends has very little influence on future earning potential. "What you do in college does make a big difference," the study reported. In fact, evidence published by Terenzini and Pascarella, in their 1991 book, *How College Affects Students*, suggests that only 1 to 2 percent of the differences in income after graduation are attributable to the specific college a student attends. But, you ask, is it not true that the name of a college can open doors and create contacts for my son? Yes, that is probably true. Friendships formed in college are likely to be lifelong. Yet, every college has an alumni network accessible to its new graduates; moreover, the door can as easily be opened by the Transylvania University graduate as it can by the Yale alum! So, to answer the question directly, doors are open to those who achieve at a high level in college—help your son pick the college that will facilitate that achievement and result in feelings of accomplishment for your son.

Question 3—We want our daughter to go to a "better" school than we did. Are we wrong?

No, and this concern is well-intentioned. Some parents' college decisions were actually made for them, either by their own parents ("you will go to the local college!") or because of finances ("we simply can't afford another school") or because college choices were simply not known, nor was there a perception that college selection involved choice. (The age of information and marketing has made college options and the information about them increase at an explosive rate.) So, looked at one way, this third question may revolve around the way parents made their own college decisions. Share with your daughter how you decided to attend the college that you did. If you did not attend college, talk with your daughter about your thoughts and dreams when you left high school.

Another aspect of this question relates to issues of prestige and goals that you may have for your daughter. Some parents so burden their children with their own unfulfilled dreams that they pressure their children into considering prestigious colleges so that they themselves will be perceived positively. Please have dreams and goals for your daughter. Share those dreams with her, and distinguish them from your own aspirations. Be careful that your student uses your perceptions only as information in the formulation of her own unique goals and aspirations. Help your daughter discover and name her talents and gifts and then point her in directions that will give her opportunities to develop. Also, work to respect the differences between you and your daughter. Do not assume your wonderful experience at a particular type of college will fit your daughter as well.

The appropriate college choice for your young person is that college where she will be able to enjoy success—an important ingredient in the development of self-esteem. Remember, it is your daughter, not you, who will spend hours and days in the classroom and in the library. Help her make those hours enjoyable and rewarding, not filled with struggle, frustration and tears, simply because she made a college decision for you, not herself. Finally, once your daughter does make a college decision, affirm her choice. Spare her from feeling guilty if she happens to make a choice that would not be yours. Help her know her choices are acceptable to you. A college choice is rarely "right" or "wrong" in the abstract. In fact, it is clear to those advising young people in college choice that adolescents really do know what is best for themselves. They will tell us, if only we will listen.

Question 4—Our son really hasn't been very successful in high school, so we don't want to spend very much for his college education. Wouldn't we just be throwing money down the drain?

At its core, this concern views the amount of money spent on college tuition as a reward or punishment for performance. While practicality may suggest this position is logical, parents are advised to view the college experience not as a product on which a price tag is affixed, but rather as a process whose benefits are without price. An inexpensive college is no more likely to provide a successful college experience for a late bloomer than an expensive one. The most important concern should be that of match and the ability of any given college environment to provide the elements, qualities, and people necessary for your son to succeed.

Question 5—How do I deal with images and perceptions about colleges?

There are so many images about colleges, and the grapevine seems to continue to work overtime! Here are a few perceptions; some stated seriously, some stated humorously:

"Only a big school can be fun."

"Without fraternities and sororities, my son will have no social life."

"The College of the Sun is a party school."

Students can have a great deal of fun at a small school; many would even contend that the *absence* of fraternities and sororities is a guarantee of a social life. No school is entirely a party school, nor is any school entirely a grind school. Students will surely find parties and grinds at every school if they seek those kinds of experiences.

"The College of the Urbanites is dangerous because it is located in a city."

"My daughter will have nothing to do at The College of the Cows because it is located in a small town."

A city is not a city is not a city (with apologies to Gertrude Stein); in short, not every urban campus is dangerous, nor every small town a bore. Small towns across the country vary a great deal, so also do the colleges that are located in them!

A common theme underlies all of these perceptions. Sometimes, perceptions are based on experience and sometimes they are based on hearsay or outdated notions. Check out perceptions you hear with reliable information. Be wary of making such blanket statements about any given school or area of the country. And be cautious about accepting such stereotypes from your son or daughter.

Question 6—My son's friend got into a very competitive college last year with lower SAT scores than my son. Yet, our counselor thought my son would likely be denied admission. Why?

Admission is a complex though not mystical process. Rarely does one factor, like SAT scores, an average letter of recommendation, or one low grade, in and of itself, cause a student to be denied or accepted. As was described in Chapter 7, college admission committees carefully and thoughtfully consider many dimensions of each applicant when they admit a class. Hence, the fact that one student was admitted one year with particular SAT scores means very little for admission of another student with another set of scores the following year. More importantly, many factors are considered, and one set of parents may not know everything about another candidate for admission the previous year. Again, the grapevine at work! Students and parents seldom know all of the details contained in another student's admission folder.

Further, the admission picture for any given school changes from year to year depending on the number of applications received for the freshman class and the qualities of the class that are sought. Most importantly, we do not know whether the college that matched a student's friend also matches the needs of your student. Importantly, too, parents should work hard to assess their student objectively in light of the criteria available from most counselors. The Admission Profile, Worksheet 4, can help you compare your student with others. While every parent would like to believe that his or her son or daughter is simply tops (and should be in your eyes), college admission committees see a young person inevitably in light of the other thousands of applications they read each year. Remember, the United States has over 20,000 high schools, each with a valedictorian. Many of those 20,000 valedictorians apply to the 100 most selective colleges in the nation.

Question 7—My daughter's counselor can't tell us what the precise requirements are for admission at a particular college. Shouldn't he know if the college requires, say, a 3.2 grade average and a combined SAT I score of 1100?

Few colleges admit by a strict formula. Most colleges weigh all of the factors previously discussed in making admission decisions. The admission decision is based on a composite of factors such as strength of the student's program, the recommendations, test scores, activities, evidence of intellectual curiosity and other factors described in Chapter 7. Your counselor, however, should be able to give you some indication of the chances for admission based on her or his experience with other students applying to that college. You, too, can assess your students' chances by reading the section titled "Concerning Your Likelihood of Admission" in Chapter 4.

YOUR PROPER LEVEL OF INVOLVEMENT

Choosing a college is a family decision, with the student in the driver's seat. In fact, parents ought to look on the college admission and decision-making process as an educational opportunity. A student who makes a college decision makes one of the most critical decisions in his or her life. Like most decisions, it should be made strategically and systematically, not serendipitiously or whimsically.

Unfortunately, many students come to the college decision with little or no experience at major decision-making. Hence, parents do their young people a very valuable service by illustrating and giving them practice at making small choices. Parents aid their students by giving them strategies for solving problems but then allowing them to take the lead in the college admission process. Students, and not parents, should make college visit arrangements, requests for applications and catalogues and, of course, be responsible for their own applications and essays. Help your young person be organized, but leave it up to him or her to establish an application timetable and meet deadlines. Yes, the process seems confusing and is, at best, complex. Each college may seem to have a different application deadline and request different documents. And even if a student can make sense out of these issues, he or she is not guaranteed admission.

Nevertheless, the college planning process presents a number of opportunities for permitting students to learn leadership and control. Importantly, too, in the context of college planning, students will gradually move from dependence to independence. And when students do not assume control or when they slip, you can help most by *not* rescuing them! Instead of taking over the process, you are of most help if you can talk through strategies with your student. Help your student learn how to address new problems as they arise. After all, once fall arrives and college registration is complete, a young person will not have a parent available at every turn or at every disappointment. Instead, they will call upon the problem-solving skills you have taught them, and be empowered to resolve a decision or a problem on their own.

The college decision is also a decision about familial values. Is a religious environment really best for your daughter? Is cost important in making the final college choice? Is it critical that your son be near relatives so that he can celebrate major holidays with extended family? Would you pay

113

more for a college you perceive as higher in status? The questions and the issues are endless. Most families leave their values unstated; the college decision-making process can change that. By working with your student on Worksheets 5 and 6 you'll find ample opportunities for discussions about the values and beliefs your family unit views as important.

Trust, openness and supportiveness are key qualities that help ease the college process. Permit your young person to try out ideas and plans on you without reacting in horror. It is common for students to have a favorite college or major each week or day of the senior year! A student may even claim that he or she is not going to go to college—often this feeling simply reflects the exasperation and anxiety felt when gathering information and making an important decision. Again, the best response is to provide an arena for a calm discussion of strategies; in the case of the young person who indicated he was not going to college, his mother engaged him in a discussion of some of the pros and cons by which he would weigh two alternatives—college and the Marines—and within a week, he decided he was still committed to attending college.

Emotions like fear, frustration, defensiveness, and anger may arise during the college planning process. By applying to college, your young person is, perhaps for the first time, holding up his or her credentials against the light of a wider base than that provided by the home high school. And putting oneself against a new background of competition often leads to fear and uncertainty. At the same time that your adolescent is making a very important decision, he or she is also deciding to leave the supportive and familiar environment of home and family. In preparing for college, a student is initiating action that causes separation and often pain. It is no surprise, then, that some students are ambivalent and procrastinate about completing their applications and, ultimately about making a decision on which college to attend. Also, it is no wonder that some feel defensive and want to be fiercely independent (gaining some early practice before leaving home). Each of these reactions is normal, human and, frankly, quite understandable. While these reactions may tax the patience and the tempers of parents, empathy and understanding will go a long way in keeping peace at home during the senior year. The year before college is one of the most poignant times for parents as they must balance their roles of separation and support. Remember, no single way of accomplishing these tasks is "best" or "right."

SOME SPECIFIC SUGGESTIONS

The previous pages dealt with broad issues and questions. But some specific suggestions may help to summarize and condense the important college planning issues for parents.

1. Assist your young person in keeping track of the college planning goals provided in Appendices A, B and C.
2. Trust your counselor and heed his or her advice. Attend programs held

at your high school concerning college planning and meet with the college counselor.

3. Encourage your son or daughter to appraise objectively his or her abilities and limitations. Consider such questions as: In which subjects does your young person excel? At what level are his or her high school classes? Which subjects are most difficult? How are his or her study skills? How well does he or she communicate, orally as well as on paper? What is your young person's experience in such classes as English, mathematics, laboratory sciences, foreign languages? How are his or her college entrance test scores?

4. Assist your student in assessing interests and preferences. Ask questions such as: About which subjects is your student passionate? What does he or she read for pleasure? What hobbies does he or she pursue? In which extracurricular activities has your student found the most enjoyment? Which jobs have been most interesting?

5. Help your student sort out the most important qualities in his or her choice of college (by reviewing Worksheets 5 and 6). As you review these qualities, you will want to arrive at consensus with your student about such issues as cost, distance from home, and religious affiliation. The best college decision you can help your young person make is one that represents the best match of a student's interests, abilities, preferences, and unique qualities with the characteristics and special features of any given college or university. The most critical consideration is choosing an academic environment in which your young person will thrive, mature, and find enjoyment as well as stimulation.

6. Be a careful, systematic, and thoughtful aid in the information-gathering and decision-making processes. Help your student use the resources listed in Chapter 4. Colleges do a lot of aggressive marketing, and while students may feel flattered by receiving all their mail and telephone calls, do not overinterpret the intent of the communication. But recognize that at some point you stop gathering *facts* and begin gathering *feelings.*

7. Encourage your son or daughter to keep his or her options open and to have many college choices. Don't focus on one college too early in the process. Your son or daughter should have at least one reach college, one competitive college, and one back-up college. All three should be fully acceptable to you. See Chapter 4 for ways of identifying these admission categories. You can be most helpful in the application completion phase (in the Fall of the Senior year) by encouraging your student to establish a target date for each application and by urging systematic completion of applications (for example, complete one application per weekend for a month). Worksheet 10 in Chapter 4 will help keep track of application steps.

8. No college is perfect and parents can help each student evaluate how he or she will cope with the inherent trade-offs among the good and bad features of each school.

9. Share with your student your own feelings, thoughts, and expectations about college and label them as such. Use your adult maturity and objectivity to be open-minded and nonjudgmental as you listen to your child. Avoid the "my sister-in-law's cousin's daughter said college Z is horrible" mentality.

10. Encourage your student to share his or her thoughts, feelings, and ideas about college. Talk about fears such as an admission denial, homesickness and how you will communicate when he or she is away from home.

11. Respect your student's desires for privacy about his or her scores, grades, and other pertinent admission information. The stress and uncertainty of college planning often brings parents of students into contact with each other, and discussions about the frustrations and excitement of college planning can be beneficial. Your student's specific scores and grade point average, however, are confidential and only he or she may choose to share them with others.

12. Finally, be aware of the language you use as you talk about college plans to others. Avoid saying "*We* are looking at small colleges," or "*We've* decided to attend State U." Your son or daughter is the one making the college choice; the plural pronoun, "we," is inappropriate and pulls the focus away from the central figure in the process, your student.

DEALING WITH REJECTION

Good college planning suggests that a student's application list should contain at least one or two "reach" schools where the likelihood of admission is slim—perhaps as low as 10-20%. Of course, the application list should also include a group of schools where the likelihood of admission (as discussed in Chapter 4) is much higher. In short, then, good counseling anticipates rejection.

Any admission denial is disappointing, and parents can help their students understand that "rejection" does not mean "unacceptable." A denial usually means a college simply had too many applications for the available spaces in its dormitories, or that the college felt (based on its experience and judgment) the student would likely not have a successful experience there.

A rejection can shatter a teenager's confidence. If expanded and repeated, it can do major damage to a student's sense of self-worth. The denial comes at a particularly difficult time in a teenager's life, a time when he or she is struggling with such issues as independence, confidence and self-worth. The acceptance is seen not only as an admission to college, but as admission to future success and ultimate happiness. Indeed, students may see acceptance to a prestigious university as a mark of value and worthiness. Do not let a college decision become a part of self-image. Also, parents can help by pointing out that admission decisions are often subjective and impersonal. Be disappointed for your student and with your student, not because of your student. Decisions reflect human judgments, and human judgments can never be infallible. For all the information colleges have about any applicant, many bits of information remain unassessed; for example, schools cannot easily quantify or evaluate motivation, creativity, and kindness. Help your student know that regardless of the decisions made by colleges, he or she is inherently and completely acceptable.

If your student is not admitted to his or her first choice, recognize the feelings your young person is facing. Dealing with setbacks is never easy, but parental attitudes play a major role in a student's emotional well-being during this period. Encourage your son or daughter to bounce back and make the most of his or her number two college choice. Since success in college is extremely important, persuade your young person to take advantage of the opportunities available at his or her second choice. Getting top grades, making a real contribution to a campus community and developing his or her people-skills will go a long way toward employment opportunities or graduate school acceptances after four years.

All students are acceptable! But if a student does receive an admission denial, parents will do well to help their student understand that such a letter is not the end of the world. Keep the process in perspective and affirm the worth of your child.

FINAL COMMENTS

Parents, your role in the process of helping your young person select a college is central and important. You will set the stage on which a crucial decision will take place. Your insights and your emotional level-headedness will contribute to the final choice.

Parents can help their students through the college choice process by promoting their children's self-understanding. Help them know themselves, their background and their values. Parents should not be expected to have vast amounts of college expertise, but they would be wise to consult an objective outsider—a counselor—for help, advice, and experienced judgment. Parents should support, respect, love, and affirm the wonderful young people they are about to help launch on their own exciting journeys.

Appendix A
College Planning Goals—Freshman and Sophomore Years

FRESHMAN YEAR

- Establish strong study habits and time management techniques.
- Develop a reading plan that includes newspapers, magazines and books.
- Learn how to use the library.
- Work to enhance your reading and writing abilities and vocabulary proficiency.
- Keep your grades up.
- Plan your sophomore year schedule with care. Take classes appropriate for you. Push yourself but know your limits. Colleges look carefully at your classes (and not just your grades). A strong college preparatory program balanced with courses in English, mathematics, social studies, science and foreign language is important.
- Investigate extracurricular activities in which you would like to participate.
- Enjoy school! And not only as a prelude to college but as a place where you are developing as a student and as a person.
- Think about your interests and how those interests might translate into career options. But keep your career options open. Investigate lots of possibilities.
- Pay attention to what friends and others are saying about their college experiences. Think about your own goals for college.
- Meet with your college counselor. Find out about college planning resources available in your school.
- Consider an interesting summer job, travel, or other learning experience.

SOPHOMORE YEAR

- Meet with your college counselor. Ask about early planning for college.
- Maintain strong study habits and time management techniques.
- Continue your reading plan, including newspapers, magazines and books.
- Work to enhance your reading and writing abilities and vocabulary proficiency. Assess your writing strengths and weaknesses and work on weaknesses.

- Keep your grades up. Keep copies of your best writing.
- Plan your junior year schedule carefully. Take classes appropriate for you: push yourself but know your limits. Colleges will look carefully at your classes (and not just your grades). A strong, college preparatory program balanced with courses in English, mathematics, social science, science and foreign language is important.
- Target major activities. Aim for leadership positions, if appropriate. Keep a record of performances/events/awards.
- Think about those qualities which would make a college right for you.
- Pay attention to what friends and others are saying about their college experiences.
- Sit in on a few meetings with college representatives who visit your school.
- Consider teachers who you would like to have write college recommendations for you.
- Some students take preliminary exams this year; the PSAT (to prepare for the SAT) or PLAN (to prepare for the ACT). Ask your counselor.
- Think about your interests and how those interests might translate into career options. But keep your options open. Investigate lots of possibilities.
- Some students take one (or more) SAT II: Subject Tests in the spring of this year if they are completing a college preparatory subject. Again, consult with your counselor about this.
- Consider an interesting summer job, travel, or other learning experience.

Appendix B
College Planning Goals—Junior Year

PREPARING FOR COLLEGE

- Relax. Approach the college search systematically.
- Keep your grades up.
- Begin/continue extracurricular involvements.
- Plan senior year schedule carefully. Push yourself, but know your limits.
- Work on study skills and time management.
- Complete Activities/Experiences Record (Worksheet 3).
- Think about several career options. Actively investigate a few.
- Consider an interesting summer job or travel experience.
- Take every opportunity to improve your writing skills.

FINDING COLLEGES AND PREPARING TO APPLY

- Meet with your high school counselor. Find out how college planning operates at your school and identify the resources available to you.
- Label a manila folder "COLLEGE PLANNING." In it, put important papers pertaining to your college search.
- Identify qualities important in college selection. Complete Worksheets in Chapter 3.
- Attend college representative meetings at school/college night programs/college fairs.
- Write colleges for viewbooks and applications. See Appendix F.
- Research college choices. See Chapter 4.
- Develop a preliminary list of colleges that interest you. Complete Worksheet 7.
- Identify and possibly talk to teachers about recommendations/college plans.
  Names of possible recommenders:

_____

_____

_____

- Begin to explore financial aid opportunities. Note resources listed in the References section of this book.
- Start work on essay preparation. See Chapter 6.
- Consider visits to college campuses—after you speak to your counselor and begin to research potential college choices. See Chapter 5.

TESTING NEEDS

- Consider test preparation such as use of sample tests or tutoring.

- PLAN Test Date_____   Registration Deadline _____

- PSAT Test Date_____   Registration Deadline _____

- SAT I Test Date_____   Registration Deadline _____

    Test Date_____   Registration Deadline _____

- ACT Test Date_____   Registration Deadline _____

    Test Date_____   Registration Deadline _____

- SAT II: Subject Tests. Under test name, list the specific tests you will take. For example, Writing, Mathematics Level I and Biology.

Test Name	Test Date	Registration Deadline
_____	_____	_____
_____	_____	_____
_____	_____	_____

SUMMER PLANS

College Planning Goals. Check those you will accomplish.

_____ Study my college options

_____ Prepare for college entrance tests

_____ Refine my list of colleges

_____ Talk with current students

_____ Write for college applications

_____ Work on my essays

_____ Visits to colleges? Where? _____

_____ Organize my list of high school activities

_____ Other. What? _____

_____ Other. What? _____

List your summer activities:

_____

_____

_____

_____

_____

_____

_____

_____

_____

_____

_____

_____

_____

_____

Appendix C
College Planning Goals—Senior Year

PREPARING FOR COLLEGE

- Keep your "cool" during this year. Systematically move from one phase of the college search to another.
- Keep your grades up. This year *is* important. Remember, many colleges will see your first semester grades.
- Begin/continue extracurricular involvements.
- Work on study skills and time management.
- Think about several career options. Actively investigate a few.
- Complete Activities/Experiences Record (Worksheet 3).
- Keep your parents informed as to your thinking about your college choices. Seek their counsel.

FINDING COLLEGES AND APPLYING

- Meet regularly with your high school college counselor.
- Identify qualities important in college selection. Complete Worksheets in Chapter 3.
- Attend college representative meetings at school/college night programs/college fairs.
- Write colleges for viewbooks and applications. See Appendix F.
- Research college choices. Narrow the field. Complete Worksheet 9.
- Use a manila file folder for each college to which you are applying. In it, put applications and other materials for that college.
- Talk to teachers about college recommendations/distribute them. Names of recommenders:

_____

_____

_____

_____

- Work systematically on your applications and essays. Find out precisely what forms, test scores, etc. are required for all of your college choices.
- Discuss applying "Early Decision" or "Early Action" with your counselor.
- Develop a timetable for application due dates. Complete Worksheet 10.
- Complete and mail applications to colleges. My target date to mail all applications is _____
- Practice for college interviews.
- Investigate all relevant scholarship possibilities. Standardized forms are available after Jan. 1. Check with each college for aid information and procedures.
- Consider the best time for college visitations. Where and When?

_____

_____

_____

- Meet housing deadlines.
- Send housing deposit and confirmation to attend.

- SAT I   Test Date _____   Registration Deadline _____

        Test Date _____   Registration Deadline _____

- ACT   Test Date _____   Registration Deadline _____

        Test Date _____   Registration Deadline _____

- SAT II: Subject Tests. Under test name, list the specific tests you will take. For example, Writing, Mathematics Level I and Biology.

Test Name	Test Date	Registration Deadline
_____	_____	_____
_____	_____	_____
_____	_____	_____

Appendix D
Possible Major Fields of Study

Agricultural Studies
Anthropology
Architecture
Arts (Fine, Visual, Performing
   and Design)
Biology
Business and Management
Chemistry
Communications
Computer and Information Sciences
Construction Trades
Economics
Education/Teaching
Engineering
English
Environmental Design
Ethnic Studies (African American,
   Asian, Hispanic, Latin-American,
   etc.)
Fashion Merchandising
Geography
Geology/Earth Sciences/
   Environmental Science
Government
Health Sciences/Allied Health
   (occupational therapy, physical
   therapy, dental assistant,
   nursing, etc.)
History
Home Economics
Interdisciplinary Studies
International Relations
Journalism
Languages
Marketing
Mathematics
Mechanics and Repairs

Military Sciences
Music
Philosophy
Physics/Physical Sciences
Political Science
Pre-Professional Studies (pre-
   engineering, pre-law, pre-med,
   pre-dental, etc.)
Protection Services (criminal justice,
   fire protection, etc.)
Psychology
Public Affairs
Religion/Theology
Sociology
Speech Communication
Theatre
Tourism Industry
Transportation (piloting, air traffic
   control, etc.)
Women's Studies

Appendix E
Potential College Activities List

ACADEMIC CLUBS .... such as English Society, Business
Students' Association, Political
Science Association, American
Society of Civil Engineers

ADMISSION OFFICE ASSISTANCE .... (tours, phone calls, policies)

ARTS CLUBS

DANCE CLUBS

DEBATE

DRAMATIC PRODUCTIONS .... such as Mime Troupe, Improvisa-
tion Troupe, Formal Theatre
Productions

FILM SERIES/CONCERT
PRODUCTIONS COMMITTEES

FRATERNITY/SORORITY

HOBBY CLUBS .... such as Amateur Radio Club,
Bridge Club, Chess Club, Photog-
raphy Club

INTERNATIONAL STUDENT
ORGANIZATIONS

JOURNALISM .... such as Newspaper, Yearbook,
Literary Magazines, other campus
publications

MUSICAL ACTIVITIES .... such as Choir, Band, Jazz Band,
Marching Band

RADIO/TELEVISION STATION

RELIGIOUS ORGANIZATIONS

SOCIAL ACTION/POLITICAL GROUPS .. such as College Democrats, College Republicans, Amnesty International, Greenpeace, Right to Life, Committee Concerned With World Hunger, Students for the Rainforest, or other community service or tutoring opportunities

SPORTS/RECREATION .... such as Varsity Sports, Intramural Sports, Bicycling, Outdoor Adventurers, Sailing, Floor-hockey, Broomball, Frisbee, Skiing, Windsurfing, Climbing Club

STUDENT GOVERNMENT/
RESIDENCE HALL GOVERNMENT

Appendix F
Requesting Information from Colleges — A Sample Postcard

SAMPLE FRONT OF POSTCARD

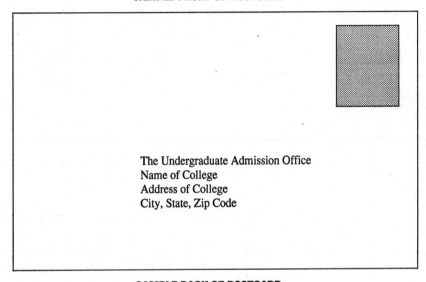

The Undergraduate Admission Office
Name of College
Address of College
City, State, Zip Code

SAMPLE BACK OF POSTCARD

Please send me information about your college. I would like an application, a Viewbook and any other pertinent information on freshman admission. Thank you.

Name

      Ms.
Mr. _____

Street _____

City, State, Zip _____

Telephone (   ) _____ Year H.S. Grad. _____
      area code

High School _____

City, State, Zip _____

Academic interest(s) _____

References For College Planning

COMPREHENSIVE GUIDEBOOKS

Barron's Profiles of American Colleges. Woodbury, New York: Barron's Educational Series, Inc. Published annually.

Cass, James and Max Birnbaum. *Comparative Guide to American Colleges.* New York: Harper & Row. Published annually.

College Admissions Index of Majors and Sports. New Orleans, LA: Wintergreen/Orchard House. Published annually.

The College Board. *The College Handbook.* New York: College Entrance Examination Board. Published annually.

The College Board. *Index of Majors and Graduate Degrees.* New York: College Entrance Examination Board. Published annually.

College Research Group of Brunswick, Maine. *The Right College.* New York: Arco Publishing. Published annually.

Lehman, Andrea E., ed. *Peterson's Guide to Four-Year Colleges.* Princeton, New Jersey: Peterson's Guides. Published annually.

Straughn, Charles T., II, and Barbarasue Lovejoy Straughn, eds. *Lovejoy's College Guide.* New York: Monarch Press. Published every few years.

SUBJECTIVE AND SPECIALIZED GUIDEBOOKS

Adler, Joe anne with Jennifer Adler Friedman. *Women's Colleges.* New York: Arco, 1994.

Antonoff, Steven R., *The College Finder,* New York: Fawcett Columbine 1993.

Borins, Sara, ed. *The Real Guide to Canadian Universities.* Toronto: Key Porter Books, 1994.

Bowman, J. Wilson, *America's Black Colleges.* South Pasadena, California: Sandcastle Publishing, 1992.

Charles, Jill, ed. *Directory of Theatre Training Programs.* Dorset, VT: Theatre Directories. Published every few years.

Consider a Christian College. Princeton: Peterson's Guides, 1988.

Everett, Carole J. *The Performing Arts Major's College Guide.* New York: Arco, 1994.

Fiske, Edward B. *The Fiske Guide To Colleges.* New York: Times Books. Published annually.

The Hillel Guide to Jewish Life on Campus. Washington, D.C.: B'nai B'rith Hillel Foundations. Published annually.

Horner, Charles, Ed., *The Common-Sense Guide to American Colleges.* New York: Madison Books, 1991.

Kravets, Marybeth and Imy F. Wax. *The K & W Guide to Colleges for the Learning Disabled.* Cambridge, MA: Educators Publishing Services, 1995.

Meltzer, Tom, Zachary Knower, Edward T. Custard and John Katzman. *The Best 306 Colleges.* New York: Villard Books. Published annually.

Miner, Brad and Charles Sykes, eds. *The National Review College Guide.* New York: Walgemuth & Hyatt, 1991.

Mitchell, Robert. *The Multicultural Students' Guide to Colleges.* New York: Noonday Press, 1993.

Nemko, Martin. *How to Get an Ivy League Education at a State University.* New York: Avon Books, 1988.

Rugg, Frederick E. *Rugg's Recommendations On The Colleges.* Atascadero, CA: Rugg's Recommendations. Published annually.

Sherrill, Jan-Mitchell and Craig A. Hardesty. *The Gay, Lesbian and Bisexual Students' Guide to the Colleges, Universities and Graduate Schools.* New York University Press, 1994.

Straughn, Charles T., *Lovejoy's College Guide for the Learning Disabled.* New York: Monarch Press, 1988.

Weinstein, Miriam, ed., *Making a Difference College Guide: Education for a Better World.* San Anselmo, California: Sage Press, 1993.

The Yale Daily News. *The Insider's Guide to the Colleges.* New York: St. Martin's Press. Published annually.

PLANNING FOR COLLEGE COSTS

Cassidy, Daniel. *The Scholarship Book.* Englewood Cliffs, New Jersey: Prentice Hall. Published annually.

The College Cost Book. New York: College Board Publications. Published annually.

College Research Group of Brunswick, Maine and John Schwartz. *College Financial Aid Annual.* New York: Arco. Published annually.

Hall, Lucy, ed. *Foundation Grants to Individuals.* New York, The Foundation Center, Published every two years.

Leider, Robert and Anna Leider. *Don't Miss Out: The Ambitious Student's Guide to Financial Aid.* Alexandria, VA: Octameron Associates. Published annually.

Santamaria, Judy K. and Oreon Keesler. *Financial Aids for Higher Education*. Dubuque, Iowa: Brown and Benchmark Publishers. Published every few years.

Wexler, Debra L., ed. *The A's and B's of Academic Scholarships*. Alexandria, Virginia: Octameron Associates. Published annually.

SUCCESS IN THE FRESHMAN YEAR

Basta, Nicholas. *Major Options*. New York: Harper Perennial, 1993.

Blumenthal, Richard A. and Joseph A. Despres. *Major Decisions: A Guide to College Majors*. New Orleans, LA: Wintergreen/Orchard House, Inc., 1992.

Ellis, David B. *Becoming a Master Student*. Rapid City, South Dakota: College Survival, 1991.

Gibbs, George. *Campus Daze: Easing the Transition From High School to College*. Alexandria, Virginia: Octameron Associates. Published every two years.

Kaye, Evelyn and Janet Gardner. *College Bound: The Student's Handbook for Getting Ready, Moving In, and Succeeding On Campus*. New York: College Board Publications, 1988.

Ostrander, Curtis and Joseph Schwartz. *Crime at College: The Student Guide to Personal Safety*. Ithaca, NY: New Strategist Publications, 1994.

Rathus, Spencer A. and Lois Fischner-Rathus. *Making the Most of College*. Englewood Cliffs, New Jersey: Prentic Hall, 1991.

Rosenberg, Ellen. *College Life*. New York: Penguin Books, 1992.

Starke, Mary C. *Survival Skills for College*, Englewood Cliffs, New Jersey: Prentice Hall, 1990.

OF INTEREST TO PARENTS

Coburn, Karen Levin and Madge Lawrence Treeger. *Letting Go: A Parent's Guide to Today's College Experience*. Bethesda, Maryland: Adler & Adler, 1988.

MacGowan, Sandra F. and Sarah M. McGinty. *50 College Admission Directors Speak to Parents*. San Diego: Harvest/Harcourt Brace Jovanovich, 1988.

Shields, Charles J. *The College Guide For Parents*. New York: College Board Publications, 1994.

GENERAL BOOKS OF INTEREST

Bauld, Harry. *On Writing the College Application Essay*. New York: Barnes & Noble Books, 1987.

Bingham, Mindy, Judy Edmondson and Sandy Stryker. *Challenges: A Young Man's Journal for Self-Awareness and Personal Planning*. Santa Barbara, California: Advocacy Press, 1993.

Bingham, Mindy, Judy Edmondson and Sandy Stryker. *Challenges: A Young Woman's Journal for Self-Awareness and Personal Planning*. Santa Barbara, California: Advocacy Press, 1993.

Curry, Boykin and Brian Kasbar, eds. *Essays That Worked*. New York: Fawcett Columbine, 1990.

Drachman van Raalte, Susan. *College Applications and Essays—A How-to Handbook*. New York: Arco, 1993.

Hayden, Thomas C., *Handbook for College Admissions*. Princeton, New Jersey: Peterson's Guides, 1989.

How to Get to the College of Your Choice: By Road, Plane or Train. Millwood, New York: Kraus International Publications, 1992.

Leider, Anna. *I Am Somebody—College Knowledge for the First Generation College Bound*. Alexandria, VA: Octameron Associates. Published every two years.

McGinty, Sarah. *Writing Your College Application Essay*. New York: College Board Publications, 1991.

National Directory of College Athletics. Cleveland, Ohio: Collegiate Directories, Inc. Published annually (both men and women's editions available).

Needle, Stacy. *The Other Route Into College: Alternative Admission*. New York: Random House, 1991.

Ordovensky, Pat and Robert Thornton. *Opening College Doors—How to Make the Admissions Process Work for You*. New York: HarperCollins, 1992.

Pope, Loren. *Looking Beyond The Ivy League*. New York: Penguin Books, 1990.

Ripple, G. Gary. *Do It Write: How to Prepare a Great College Application*. Alexandria, Virginia: Octameron Associates. Published every two years.

Spencer, Janet and Sandra Maleson. *The Complete Guide to College Visits*. New York: Citadel Press, 1993.